Lionel Sotheby's Great War

Lionel Sotheby c. 1915
Courtesy of Liddle Collection

Lionel Sotheby's Great War

Diaries and Letters from the Western Front

EDITED AND WITH AN INTRODUCTION
BY
Donald C. Richter

FOREWORD BY
Peter H. Liddle

OHIO UNIVERSITY PRESS
ATHENS

Ohio University Press, Athens, Ohio 45701
Introduction and Notes © 1997 by Donald C. Richter
Printed in the United States of America

Ohio University Press books are printed on acid-free paper ∞™

01 00 99 98 97 5 4 3 2 1

Library of Congress Cataloging-in-Publication Data
Sotheby, Lionel, 1895–1915.
   Lionel Sotheby's Great War : diaries and letters from the Western
Front / edited with an introduction by Donald C. Richter : Foreword
by Peter Liddle.
      p. cm.
   Includes index.
   ISBN 0-8214-1178-0
   1. Sotheby, Lionel, 1895–1915—Correspondence. 2. Sotheby,
Lionel, 1895–1915—Diaries. 3. World War, 1914–1918—Personal
narratives, British. 4. Great Britain. Army—Biography. 5. World
War, 1914–1918—Campaigns—France. 6. Soldiers—Great Britain—
Biography. I. Richter, Donald. C., 1934-   II. Title.
D640.S684   1997
940.4′81—dc21   96-6568
                                  CIP

Contents

Foreword / vii
List of Maps / xi
1915 Calendar / xii
Acknowledgments / xiii
Introduction / xv
A Note on the Transcription / xxv

The Diary and Letters

1 /	Crossing to France	1
2 /	With the Black Watch at Le Havre	4
3 /	Painful Journey	26
4 /	Just Behind the Front Lines	34
5 /	Pills and Ills	49
6 /	Mock Bombing Attacks	54
7 /	Into the Trenches for the First Time	75
8 /	The Battle of Neuve Chapelle	81
9 /	Aubers Ridge	97
10 /	More Narrow Escapes	108
11 /	Ambushed in a Listening Post	115
12 /	Straining to Go	123

The Battle of Loos: "Action at Piètre" / 135
Epilogue / 139
Index / 145

FOREWORD

At the very heart of my work as a historian and archivist is the sense of satisfaction at the rescue of original personal experience material that might otherwise have been lost. The Sotheby letters and diaries offer a prime example of where that sense of satisfaction becomes one of exultation. Let me explain the context of such an exceptional endorsement. Three things have governed my academic work over the last thirty-two years. In combination they have produced an archive and they have found further expression in a number of books, television serials, and other audiovisual productions. Of those three things: first, I have sought evidence documenting personal experience in almost every aspect of what many still call the Great War. Second, I have tried to gather that evidence into an archive where it could be assured of long-term preservation. Third, I have studied the evidence separately, collectively, and comparatively to try to reach an understanding of what it was like to live through those years.

Every set of letters will have interwoven elements, some particular to the writer and some common to the evidence of others describing related experience. Just occasionally one man's papers capture individuality and kinship in a quite extraordinary manner. We have such a case laid out for our delight in this book: the letters and diaries of Lionel Frederick Southwell Sotheby, a junior officer serving with a famous Scottish regiment, the Black Watch, in France in 1915.

May I introduce first the Collection from which the Sotheby papers have been chosen. It is held in the Brotherton Library of the University of Leeds in the north of England and documents the experience of approximately seven thousand men and women as they lived through or died during the First World War. For any one man there may be his original letters and diaries, his photographs, official papers, art sketches, maps, three-dimensional souvenirs, perhaps his uniform and his recollections in manuscript, typescript, or tape-recorded form. There are four thousand tape-recorded interviews. This collection, the Liddle Collection, has significant holdings on Britain's 19th Century Wars and a rapidly growing section on the Second World War, currently holding about a thousand sets of papers.

Soldiers, sailors, airmen, women in various roles, civilians, workers, parents, children, pacifists and then-allies, enemies—all are represented. Quite apart from the sheer volume of material, what additionally draws scholars from far and wide to work in Leeds is the manner in which the archive is catalogued and cross-referred. Listings make it easy for researchers to find material related not just to campaigns, such as Gallipoli, or units, such as the 7th Battalion Durham Light Infantry or No. 56 Squadron Royal Flying Corps or HMS *Lion*, but to hundreds of topics, such as lice, wounds, entertainment, sniping, trench conditions, officer-man relations, discipline, the Battle of Cambrai. For the Home Front, the range of topics includes patriotism, fund-raising, munitions, food shortages, hospitals, music, and nursing. However, more unusual is that the expressions of opinion or striking of attitudes can also be cross-referred fully from contemporary letters or diaries. Soldiers' views on the enemy or on living among French or Belgian peasants, as well as reactions to the reports of strikes by shipyard workers or to the stance of conscientious objectors, are easily traceable. Similarly, the impact of the war on a man's faith, his judgment of politicians, and many more matters, like press reporting of the war, have been selected for topic cross-reference in the Collection's catalogues.

It was when an American scholar—Donald Richter from Athens, Ohio—was researching in Leeds his study of the British Special Brigade using Gas Warfare on the Western Front in 1915 through 1918 that we discussed the possibility of his considering one exceptional set of papers and preparing them for monograph publication. Donald was already, as might be expected, committed to the Western Front, so this defined his field. The man he would choose must have served in France or Belgium. Given the large body of original material necessary, it was likely that he would be an officer; not certain, but likely. He would demonstrably have to have had a keenly observant eye for detail, the capacity to capture personal relationships, to have felt and conveyed convincing emotional response to a range of circumstances. It would help if there were evidence of a sense of humor, of closeness to those to whom his letters were addressed. If he had also experienced high drama, not once but several times; if he had written with a consciousness of high purpose, of the preciousness of life, and if the fulfillment of his responsibilities had put that life regularly at risk, then here indeed Richter would have a special case, one to share with the reader eighty years after the events being described. One man among several candidates met these criteria superbly well and, sadly, offered still more—Lionel Sotheby, whose letters and diaries bring him to life as a cheerful, brave, young officer and devoted son, proud of his school, and utterly convinced of his nation's cause, was to lose his life for that cause, leading his men in battle.

In France, Sotheby's active service was with the First Battalion of the Black Watch, a Highland Regiment. The battalion was in support of the first major British offensive in 1915, the Battle of Neuve Chapelle (10–13 March). Central rather than peripheral involvement was to be the battalion's role in the Battle of Aubers Ridge (from 9 May), its grievous losses gaining no tangible reward.

Lionel's diary, commencing at the end of December 1914, soon reveals the man. He writes of getting very little sleep and suffering "horrible shivers" betokening a possible collapse of his health; he hopes "to goodness [he] shall not fall sick and get invalided back, as that would be too awful." He recovers but injures a thumb seriously. He records that there is a good deal of snow and "things look rotten, but I was never in better spirits."

In February, he learns of the death of several of his friends. He feels their loss but at the same time, as for being in khaki in France, "I am revelling in it and would not have peace declared for any money. It's simply heavenly this life." Such a statement, difficult as it may be for us to digest, is given more weight by Lionel's evident awareness of man's mortality, his own mortality. "I cannot imagine people being fed up, it's glorious, and yet I somehow feel I am living in a sort of heaven at times which may be rudely shattered at any minute."

One is bound to ask whether he were still to be reveling in it when doing spells in frontline trenches or, more particularly, taking part in a battle such as Aubers Ridge. No, that could hardly be the case, but in a letter describing the fate of the brigade ahead of the Black Watch and then of his own battalion ("15 officers killed & wounded" and "500 men killed & wounded") he writes of the immediate aftermath: "Our sensations were odd. It had been one day of disappointment & muddle in a sense, but every man was ready for a similar fate as befell the others in the morning."

In penciled or penned words, the original documents reveal a man of compelling attraction recounting an enthralling story as it unfolds. The eighty and more intervening years distancing us from the events simply dissolve as the writer gives us vivid pictures of life in and out of the front line and in battle. The resilience common to officers and men in harshly demanding circumstances is sharply delineated. There is humor and cheerfulness, unfailing patriotism, thoughtfulness and sensitivity, all of this rendered the more poignant by the recurrent expression of premonitions of personal doom. If the reader's eyebrows were to be raised by the juxtaposition of cheerfulness and the anticipation of death, then it may be added that the latter clearly inspires

Sotheby further toward the conviction that nothing but his best is good enough: to fail the highest examination of life would be to fail something far more important than any test at his beloved Eton.

The whole story, the most dramatic of dramas and most tragic of tragedies, is as inspiring as it is sad. Authenticity of factual reporting within the vision of the man himself is beyond dispute. A rigorous editor has checked the Battalion's War Diary at the Public Record Office.

When Sotheby writes: "Today I lost Corpl. Gibbs of my platoon. He was a good man & trustworthy. Poor fellow. Got his cheek & jaw torn away, also teeth & part of tongue. He was most stoic as indeed are all the Black Watch as a whole," we see an officer closely identified with his own men. We can share too his private fears, in particular of mice, concerning which he has a disturbing nightmare. His conduct before his men and facing more lethal enemies seems to have been beyond reproach: stalwart, ever cheerful and encouraging, slow to find fault and quick with a kind thought or action.

The editor's research enables him to reconstruct the circumstances of Lionel's death at the September Battle of Loos. Here, in tribute to the young officer and with thanks for the scholarship that brings his story before us, I quote from a letter written, "To my parents, school, dear Friends and Brother," by Lionel himself on 4 June 1915 and to be opened only in the event of his death. His letter draws particular attention to the men in the ranks:

> Never have such wonderful and heroic private soldiers assembled in such masses as today. To die with such is an honour. To die for one's school is an honour. To die for the safety of one's home is an honour. To die for one's country is an honour. But to die for right and fidelity is a greater honour than these. And so I feel it now.

What more needs to be written in this foreword except my congratulations to the editor and my encouragement to the reader? Read this book and be both fascinated and humbled by its witness to the triumph of human spirit in the midst of tragedy.

Peter H. Liddle, F.R. Hist.S.
The Liddle Collection, Brotherton Library
University of Leeds, April 1996

Maps

Endpapers: Lionel's hand-drawn map of the front lines at Neuve
   Chapelle
1. Lionel's hand-drawn map of Le Havre   6
2. The northern section of the Western Front in 1915   32
3. Béthune (support) area   35
4. Lionel's hand-drawn plan of Béthune and Linette's café   37
5. Action at Piètre, 25 September 1915   136

1915

January
S	M	T	W	T	F	S
					1	2
3	4	5	6	7	8	9
10	11	12	13	14	15	16
17	18	19	20	21	22	23
24	25	26	27	28	29	30
31						

February
S	M	T	W	T	F	S
	1	2	3	4	5	6
7	8	9	10	11	12	13
14	15	16	17	18	19	20
21	22	23	24	25	26	27
28						

March
S	M	T	W	T	F	S
	1	2	3	4	5	6
7	8	9	10	11	12	13
14	15	16	17	18	19	20
21	22	23	24	25	26	27
28	29	30	31			

April
S	M	T	W	T	F	S
				1	2	3
4	5	6	7	8	9	10
11	12	13	14	15	16	17
18	19	20	21	22	23	24
25	26	27	28	29	30	

May
S	M	T	W	T	F	S
						1
2	3	4	5	6	7	8
9	10	11	12	13	14	15
16	17	18	19	20	21	22
23	24	25	26	27	28	29
30	31					

June
S	M	T	W	T	F	S
		1	2	3	4	5
6	7	8	9	10	11	12
13	14	15	16	17	18	19
20	21	22	23	24	25	26
27	28	29	30			

July
S	M	T	W	T	F	S
				1	2	3
4	5	6	7	8	9	10
11	12	13	14	15	16	17
18	19	20	21	22	23	24
25	26	27	28	29	30	31

August
S	M	T	W	T	F	S
1	2	3	4	5	6	7
8	9	10	11	12	13	14
15	16	17	18	19	20	21
22	23	24	25	26	27	28
29	30	31				

September
S	M	T	W	T	F	S
			1	2	3	4
5	6	7	8	9	10	11
12	13	14	15	16	17	18
19	20	21	22	23	24	25
26	27	28	29	30		

October
S	M	T	W	T	F	S
					1	2
3	4	5	6	7	8	9
10	11	12	13	14	15	16
17	18	19	20	21	22	23
24	25	26	27	28	29	30
31						

November
S	M	T	W	T	F	S
	1	2	3	4	5	6
7	8	9	10	11	12	13
14	15	16	17	18	19	20
21	22	23	24	25	26	27
28	29	30				

December
S	M	T	W	T	F	S
			1	2	3	4
5	6	7	8	9	10	11
12	13	14	15	16	17	18
19	20	21	22	23	24	25
26	27	28	29	30	31	

Acknowledgments

Greatest thanks go to Peter Liddle, who kindly allowed me access to the Liddle Collection at the University of Leeds, and to Mrs. Diana Fry, who donated the Sotheby Papers and subsequently granted permission for me to undertake the task of editing. My wife, Jane, patiently proofread the manuscript and contributed invaluable editing suggestions. Abigail Burnworth and the Instructional Media and Technology Services at Ohio University worked computer wonders to create the maps to my specifications. Thanks to our Welsh friend Ann Maitland whose sleuthing helped to authenticate the location, spelling, and present status of Lionel's Anglesey home territory and to her husband Norman for a pleasant afternoon's chauffeuring around the area. Barry Thomas, a good friend and colleague in the German Department, generously lent his expertise in deciphering Lionel's sometimes strangulated attempts at the language of the enemy.

INTRODUCTION

Seldom does the Great War historian searching for human interest find a collection of soldier's papers of such compelling drama as those of young Lionel Sotheby. These handwritten diaries and letters reveal an extraordinary wealth of information, not only about the many hazards and tribulations of life in the frontline trenches, but also about the day-to-day life of a second lieutenant—lack of bathing facilities, difficulties of communication with French shopkeepers, illnesses, leaking tents, bicycle misadventures, paying for haircuts, batman* problems, parcels from home, the censoring of letters; there is little of army life during the Great War that cannot be found here in engrossing personal detail.

Lionel Frederick Southwell Sotheby was the eldest son of Margaret and William Edward Southwell Sotheby of the Welsh village of Dwyran on the Isle of Anglesey, North Wales. Included in the postal address was the nearby town of Llanfairpwllgwyngyllgogerychwyrndrobwllllantysiliogogogoch,† the longest town name in Great Britain, which appears on the address of most of Lionel's letters home as Llanfair P.G., a common and understandable shortening. Set on the banks of the Menai Strait on the outskirts of Dwyran, the family farm boasted a commanding view of Caernarfon Castle across the water. The site of the large house, named Menaifron ("Menai view"), has become a block of flats. He came from a family long distinguished for public as well as military service. The family name, prominent as early as the fifteenth century, originated in Birdsall, Yorkshire, but since 1780 the family seat has been at Ecton, Northamptonshire. The first William Sotheby on the family tree below, Lionel's great-great-grandfather, was a colonel in the Coldstream Guards. One of his sons, also named William S., was a noted author and literary figure active in the Dilettante Society and a friend of Byron, Scott, Coleridge, Arthur Hallam, and Wordsworth. He also served in the Dragoons from 1774 to 1780. His son, Charles, was a rear admiral in the navy. In the 1880s, Charles's son, Charles William Hamilton Sotheby, became high sheriff of Northamptonshire.

---

* A batman is a servant to a British military officer.

† Mary's Church in a Hollow by the White Hazel near the Rapid Whirlpool by the Church of St. Tysilio at the Red Cave.

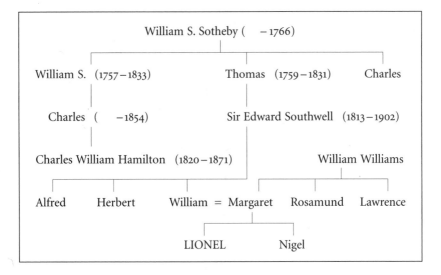

William S. Sotheby (– 1766)

William S. (1757–1833)   Thomas (1759–1831)   Charles

Charles (–1854)   Sir Edward Southwell (1813–1902)

Charles William Hamilton (1820–1871)   William Williams

Alfred   Herbert   William = Margaret   Rosamund   Lawrence

LIONEL   Nigel

Thomas Sotheby, Lionel's great-grandfather, was an admiral in the navy, while Thomas's brother Charles served as a captain, also in the navy. In the next generation, Thomas's son, Sir Edward Southwell Sotheby, C.B., K.C.B. (married to Lucy Adeane) had perhaps the most distinguished naval career of anyone in the family. He commanded the Pearl Naval Brigade during the Indian Mutiny, was mentioned in Despatches (i.e., named for special commendation) thirteen times, rose to admiral in 1879, and served as extra aide-de-camp to Queen Victoria. Upon his death in 1902 he was buried on the family estate at Ecton. His first son was Lionel's father, William E. S. Sotheby. Lionel also had two uncles on this side of the family, Herbert (unmarried) and Alfred (married to Barbara Leighton).

Lionel's mother was Margaret Williams, and on this side of the family nicknames seem to abound, so that Rosamund (unmarried) appears in the correspondence as Aunt Dodie, Lawrence as Uncle Bootie, and his wife Henrietta as Aunt Hennie.

At the time of Lionel's birth in 1895 the family was living at Cippenham House in Burnham, Buckinghamshire, just on the outskirts of London. The next year the family moved to Sussex Lodge, Slough, and later to North Wales, where the family was residing when the Great War erupted in August 1914.

The Sotheby family became much involved in the war effort, the father serving in the British Red Cross Society as a Motor Ambulance chauffeur, stationed in France at Boulogne-sur-Mer and during the latter part of the war in the Balkans. Lionel's younger brother, Nigel W. A. Sotheby, served with the Dover Patrol aboard HMS *Matchless* and HMS *Brittania* and rose to the rank of lieutenant commander. Nigel's future wife, Doris Lees, worked as a Red Cross VAD (Volunteer Aid Detachment) ambulance driver. Doris and Nigel were married in 1925, and it is their daughter, Mrs. Diana Fry, who has so graciously presented the wartime papers of her parents and those of her Uncle Lionel for preservation in the Liddle Collection.

Lionel's uncle Captain Herbert George Sotheby was a career army officer, having joined up in 1902, and was by the outbreak of the war a captain in the 2nd Battalion of the Argyll and Sutherland Highlanders. After recovering from wounds suffered in France in November 1914, he served in various capacities and in 1916 achieved the rank of lieutenant colonel in command of the 10th Battalion, which he commanded for the duration of the war. He later published his unit's wartime regimental history, *10th Battalion, Argyll and Sutherland Highlanders 1914-1919* (London, 1931). The regiment is perhaps best known through the writing of one of its other early members, Ian Hay, whose reminiscence *The First Hundred Thousand* remains immensely popular.

Lionel himself, following youthful years at Langley, went on to Eton, where he joined the Eton College Officers Training Course (Army Class) like most boys enrolled there. Although membership was technically voluntary, peer pressure in those days made joining the ECOTC almost mandatory. Most officers in the British Army came from about ten public schools—Eton, Harrow, Winchester, and Wellington heading the list. Lionel's father had been an Etonian, leaving in 1883, and as enrollment tended to foster inherited loyalty, it was not uncommon that both Sotheby boys, Lionel and Nigel, should also enroll at the school. They shared the same house, headed by P. Williams. It was at Eton that a close friendship developed between the Sotheby boys and another Eton student, Algernon Belmont, who appears occasionally in Lionel's letters as does Algernon's sister, Elaine. Eton's headmaster at the time was Rev. the Hon. Edward Lyttelton, D.D.

After Lionel's death the *Eton College Chronicle* was to write somewhat curiously:

> Though he played football hard, rowed hard, and worked conscientiously, he was not distinguished at Eton as an athlete, nor had he more than average brains. There was indeed nothing special about his Eton career to reveal what lay below, and even his closest friends can hardly have realized the depth of his faith or the intensity of his love for Eton and Eton's honour.[*]

---

[*] *Eton College Chronicle,* 21 October 1915, p. 900.

Repeated diary references to Eton indicate how much the years spent there had in fact influenced Lionel. Indeed he remained almost as affectionately devoted and loyal to the school as to his family. He left Eton at the end of third term, Christmas 1913, at which time he decided to seek civil employment in business. To better prepare himself for such a career, he spent seven months studying German at the Institute Tilly in Berlin, returning to England in mid-July, 1914. At home in the aristocratic world of London clubs, he frequented Boodle's, Brooks's, the Carleton, and other fashionable establishments. When Britain declared war on Germany several weeks later, although Lionel still had no intention of making the army a career, he signed up without hesitation. Not surprisingly he joined his uncle's regiment, the Argyll and Sutherland High-landers. Records of the 4th Battalion show his name leading a list of eighteen officers who signed up on 15 August 1914.

The letters in this collection begin in mid-1914 and the first of his wartime diaries shortly after his joining the battalion. The vast majority of the letters are to his mother at home in North Wales or to his father in France. A few are to aunts and uncles with instruction to pass them along to other family members and intimate family friends. Most letters close with "Your affectionate son," and in the curious but then-common style, Lionel occasionally signs with both Christian and family names.

Far from a dreary account of misery and tragedy, Lionel's writing exudes a wry sense of humor and excitement. He is able to tell a story with both warmth and spontaneity. His style is refreshingly unaffected and ingenuous, and he recounts embarrassing tales unabashedly. One of the most attractive features of the account is Lionel's ability to poke fun at himself. With self-ef-facing chagrin he writes of getting his cumbersome gear on in the cramped confines of a tent and then not being able to get out of the tent. It is not only the stories that are funny, but the amusing turns of phrase Lionel employs, as "My first pair [of boots] were unlucky as I lost them." He describes baggage carts as "looking awfully fed up," and his wounded thumb as "bored with life" (the modern reader may not recognize the then-current connotation of *bored* as "annoyed" or "irritated," a usage that Lionel employs frequently).

Both the letters and diaries present an introspective young man of a philosophical tendency, someone who ponders reflectively the eerie incongru-ity of idyllic scenery and the killing taking place nearby. He shows himself singularly sentimental, with an eye alert for the beautiful scene, for aesthet-ics—a sensitive young man easily moved by poetry, remarking frequently that some trifle will remain precious to him always. He is perhaps a little naive, easily impressed.

The twenty-year-old Lionel is affable and outgoing and he makes friends easily. He is enthusiastic in his youth and imbued with an appealing sense of duty and patriotism. Here is a junior officer who invariably finds charitable excuses for the shortcomings of his men and batmen, some of whom seem unconscionably inept. He has a good word for virtually everyone; he is rarely critical. Uncommonly tolerant of the faults of others and exhibiting an unusually forgiving nature, Lionel nevertheless sets an unusually high standard of conscientiousness for himself. A product of his generation and class, he displays, however, a keen disapproval of lower-class French, blacks, and Indians, whose actions he unvaryingly disparages.

Chivalrous almost to a fault, Lionel the amiable young lieutenant invariably adopts a polite and gentlemanly attitude to the few women he meets. He is the sort of young man who disapproves of "fast French girls" but is attracted to girls like Linette, whom he encounters at an estaminet in Béthune, and whom he describes as "demure, quiet and decent."

Unlike so many postwar reminiscences of grievance, this is not a whining complaint, but rather a healthy exuberant account written by a young soldier exhilarated by danger. He describes annoyances and mishaps without the slightest suggestion of serious exasperation or complaint. Clearly unsympathetic to pacifists or malingerers, Lionel's youthful courage is almost palpably felt. Far from aspiring for the Blighty wound that sends so many others homeward, Lionel seems to luxuriate in the discomforts and perils of military life. Most remarkable, although deeply moved and saddened when brought face-to-face with samples of war's most gruesome horrors, he remains undaunted, even exuberant, rarely discouraged or dispirited. The most macabre scenes of mutilated or decomposing bodies fail to dampen Lionel's indomitable spirit. In spite of all hardships, he remains cheerful, eager to advance and confront the enemy, no matter the personal sacrifice. It is a noble selfless sentiment far more rare in today's less "patriotic" world, but a virtue that characteristically animated most products of the public schools of that generation.

With that singular insensitivity to parental concern so typical of youth, Lionel writes excitedly to his mother and father of his narrow escapes, apparently oblivious of the probable effect on them. His description of the sudden death of a comrade shot through the head by sniper fire while standing inches away from him spares no gory detail.

At the same time, Lionel occasionally ponders the larger questions of tactics and strategy. For example, whichever side advances is mowed down in withering fire. Simple attack across defended trenches is worse than futile. In several rambling paragraphs on military theory, he expostulates on such topics as the importance of superior forces, intelligence, the element of surprise, morale, weather conditions, and the battle terrain.

The regiment Lionel first joined, the Argyll and Sutherland Highlanders, was descended from two Scottish clan regiments of the eighteenth century, the 91st Argylls and the 93rd Sutherlands, which in 1881 became the 1st and 2nd Battalions respectively of the renamed Argyll and Sutherland Highlanders. The regiment's honorary colonel-in-chief was HRH Princess Louise, fourth daughter of Queen Victoria, who had married the Duke of Argyll. At the outbreak of the war various Scottish militia formed into successive regimental battalions, among which was the 4th, Lionel's battalion, and to which were still later added Kitchener's New Army battalions (including Uncle Herbert's later command, the 10th Battalion). Lionel began his military adventures as a lowly subaltern in A Company, No. 2 Platoon.

On 5 October the 4th Battalion arrived at Crownhill Hutments at Devonport for the start of training. Three days later Uncle Herbert embarked for Belgium. After six weeks of training, about which Lionel writes almost nothing, the battalion on 17 November left Devonport for Newcastle, where for another six weeks the raw troops continued training, practiced digging trenches, and helped patrol a section of the Sunderland North Sea coast. On the last day of December 1914, together with a friend, Captain Nicol,* Lionel finally embarked for France. It was at this point that Lionel began to write his five-month-long personal diary.

Before leaving Southampton, perhaps in the wee hours of the night and beset by powerful premonitions of death, Lionel wrote and sent to the Sotheby family solicitor a sealed note containing a strangely disordered last will disposing of many of his personal belongings and with instructions that it be opened only at his death.

Following a queasy crossing of the channel, Lionel disembarked at the cobbled-street port of Le Havre, at the mouth of the River Seine (CHAPTER 1). Along with Boulogne, the town became the chief transit port for most British troops sailing to and from Southampton. Le Havre experienced a large population surge during the war, as the Belgian government set up its temporary headquarters there, as did many wartime agencies, such as the Red Cross Hospital to which Lionel's father was attached. Most newly arriving officers sought initial accommodation in hotels, and Lionel stayed his first night at Negotiant's Hôtel, afterward posted to No. 9 Camp, No. 1 Infantry Base Depot,

---

* Captain Randall J. Nicol.

one of sixteen camps near the town of Harfleur, about six and a half miles inland from Le Havre.

It was at Le Havre that Lionel learned he was to leave the Argylls and be attached to the 2nd Battalion of the Black Watch. Scotland's original Highland regiment, the Black Watch was raised in 1725 as the 42nd Regiment of Foot. The Forty-twos, as they were frequently called, were the only Scotsmen at that time legally permitted to carry arms. In 1739 the six original companies formed the regiment known as Am Freicheadan Dubh, the Black Watch—*black* for the dark color of the tartan they wore and *watch* for their duty of keeping watch over the Highlands. For the first time they constituted a Regular British Army unit. As late as 1739 all members had to be natives of Scotland. The regiment added three more companies in 1745. Upon return to Scotland in 1775 after a tour of thirty years in America, the regiment permitted the first Englishmen to join, although Gaelic continued to be spoken exclusively in the mess until the nineteenth century, and the regiment remained overwhelmingly Scottish until the twentieth century (over 88 percent as late as 1913). The Royal Highlanders fought in virtually every major British campaign of the eighteenth and nineteenth centuries—Brooklyn and Brandywine in the American War of Independence, Alexandria to Waterloo in the Napoleonic Wars, Alma River in the Crimea, the Indian Mutiny, the Relief of Khartoum in 1885, and the Boer War.

During the Cardwell reorganization of 1881, the Forty-twos became linked with the Duke of Wellington's Old 73rd (Perthshire) Regiment of Foot, the former constituting the 1st Battalion and the latter the 2nd Battalion. As its honorary colonel-in-chief, the Black Watch boasted the king himself.

The coming of the Great War found the 2nd Battalion in India as part of the 21st (Bareilly) Brigade, 7th (Meerut) Division. The battalion shipped to France, arriving in October, and went into action at Givenchy. It was to remain in the province of Artois for most of 1915.

Lionel spent four weeks under tent in the Harfleur camp waiting to join his new unit, visiting Le Havre regularly, and avidly committing to his diary everything that happened to him (CHAPTER 2).

On 27 January Lionel embarked on an uncomfortable three-day train trip to Béthune, a journey made particularly painful because of a fall in which he severely injured his thumb (CHAPTER 3).

It was upon arrival at Béthune the last days of January that Lionel discovered he was transferred from the 2nd Battalion to the 1st (by mistake, as it later turned out). The 1st Battalion of the Black Watch had been in France since mid-August, having fought at Mons, the Marne, the Aisne, First Ypres, and had been in the front lines at Festubert throughout the winter. It had suffered particularly severe losses (6 officers and 205 men) in holding the line at Givenchy during a fierce German attack on 25 January and the subsequent British counterattack and had just come out of the line for a three-week rest when Lionel arrived with a draft of fifty men (CHAPTER 4).

Béthune and its environs constituted a major staging area for British troops in Artois, the nearby villages of Mazingarbe, Burbure, Beuvry, Chocques, Annequin, and others affording convenient reserve-line billets. The La Bassée Canal marked the dividing line between British and French forces until the extension of the British sector southward later in 1915.

The 1st Battalion found billets at the ancient village of Burbure, where it awaited further much-needed replacements for the recent losses and where it would remain until the end of the month. Lionel managed to visit the far larger town of Béthune fairly regularly and it was during this time that he chanced to meet Linette, a French girl who made an exceptional impression on him. He also witnessed for the first time first-hand evidence of the damage exacted by German artillery, and he refers to the shells in the usual Tommy vernacular. A Jack Johnson was a German 17-inch shell, named after the American prizefighter, the first Negro world heavyweight champion (he defeated James Jeffries in 1910). A Black Maria was a similarly large German shell, named after the black smoke produced by its explosion. Only slightly smaller shells were called coalboxes, and still smaller shells were commonly called pip-squeaks or whiz-bangs. Lionel's initial contact with war's violence and increasing proximity to danger seems to have had such an exhilarating effect on him that he is able to describe these early experiences just behind the front lines as "glorious."

A day after writing these words Lionel came down sick and though not hospitalized, lay in bed for four days with a high temperature and aching symptoms of flu (CHAPTER 5).

For most of the month of February, the battalion conducted route marches, practiced mock battles, and began serious training in bomb (grenade) throwing, which Lionel describes in graphic detail, adding that he was enjoying himself immensely (CHAPTER 6).

On 28 February Lionel's unit relieved a battalion of Gurkhas in the front lines at Festubert, Lionel's first introduction to the front line trenches (CHAPTER 7). The British trenches in this part of Artois ran through the lowlands of the Lys Valley, while the Germans were dug in on the higher Aubers Ridge. The marshy ground made deep trenches impossible and instead the British front-line parapet was raised by sandbags, which Lionel variously terms breastworks or ramparts. In places only small platoon-manned trench posts, called Grouse

Butts, were possible. In spite of a week of stomachaches, diarrhea, and appallingly wet trench conditions, Lionel finds his work strangely exhilarating.

The Battle of Neuve Chapelle, the first independent British offensive of the war, began on 10 March and lasted three days (CHAPTER 8). Although only the 2nd Battalion went over the top in assault, Lionel's 1st Battalion saw a great deal of action both in support roles and in opposing a German counterattack. On 12 March, after two weeks on the front lines, the Coldstream Guards relieved Lionel's unit, and he and his company returned to reserve areas at Le Touret. Still "sublimely happy," Lionel writes of increasingly perilous narrow escapes and escalating dangers. Following the long account of the battle of Neuve Chapelle, Lionel stopped writing in a diary. As he later wrote, "it is quite impossible to keep a diary and letters are just as good." His letters continue uninterrupted the thread of his experiences and are as graphically descriptive as the diary.

In April Lionel went on leave, his first since going to France. Curiously the Official War Diary mentions neither his departure nor return to the regiment, but normal officers' leave was for ten days and Lionel's was in all likelihood taken sometime during the last part of April.

Lionel returned to the lines just in time for the battle of Aubers Ridge on 9 May, which is illustrated by several graphic letters (CHAPTER 9). A letter to his brother Nigel describes the failed British attack in the morning. Another to his mother describes his own harrowing experience in the afternoon attack, during which he was pinned down directly in front of the German trenches for several hours. Several interesting letters sent about this time to Lionel's father reflect the keen regard felt for Lionel by close family friends: Mr. P. Williams, tutor at Eton and one of Lionel's closest confidants; Mr. Willoughby Pemberton, another close family friend; and Edward Lyttelton, the headmaster at Eton during Lionel's attendance there.

The near escape on 9 May may have once again stirred premonitions of impending death and prompted Lionel to write and sign a poignant farewell letter dated 4 June, which he entrusted to the care of Mr. Pemberton, to be opened only on the occasion of his death, described on the outside of the sealed envelope, "On the occasion of my attaining even greater happiness."

Following the losses suffered by the 1st Battalion at Aubers Ridge, the battalion moved back to Béthune and Beuvry for reorganization and the arrival of replacement manpower. In late May the battalion spent several days up the line in relief of the 1st Cameron Highlanders. The first ten days of June were spent in reserve areas near Béthune, but on the evening of 10 June the battalion relieved the 2nd Battalion Royal Munster Fusiliers at Cuinchy on the south side of the La Bassée Canal. The Canadians, on the north side of the canal, put in an attack on the 15th, eliciting a large artillery barrage as well as rifle and sniper fire from the other side that engulfed Lionel's unit just to the south of the Canadians. It was during this bombardment that Lionel experienced his narrowest escape to that time (CHAPTER 10). The fact that Lionel's unit was located in support areas did not diminish the danger from enemy shells; if anything, that danger increased, as the enemy's biggest and most destructive shells were aimed not at the front lines, where shortfalls might injure their own men, but toward the British rear areas. It was here that Lionel described the destruction of a kitchen the unit had just been using.

Lionel received a second leave in July returning to France on 29 July to discover he had been transferred once more to the 2nd Battalion (CHAPTER 11). As part of the Bareilly Brigade (Indian Corps), this battalion had seen plenty of frontline trench service in early July and was just on the point of returning again to the front line at the time of Lionel's transfer. His August letters describe two particularly "beastly" misadventures, one being surrounded in no-man's-land, and the other a bicycle mishap.

On 24 August, after six days' rest, Lionel went back into the trenches opposite Aubers Ridge for the last time (CHAPTER 12). The British Army was now preparing in earnest for the big autumn offensive at Loos in concert with the French attack at Champagne. On 2 September Lionel resumed the diary composition he had abandoned in June. Much in his last letters and diary entries concern his state of mind as he anticipates what he expects to be a climactic affair, "the biggest battle in the world's history," after which few of the combatants will emerge unscathed.

On 24 September, the eve of his last battle, Lionel posted two letters, one to a friend, Gladys Farrow, and the other to his father (postmarked at the Field Post Office on the 24th and 25th respectively). Both letters announced that he was going over the top in the first wave in the morning "cheerful and full of hope."

The final chapter, based on information in the unit history of the Black Watch and official War Diaries, attempts to reconstruct exactly what happened to Lionel in the morning hours of 25 September 1915, the beginning of the Battle of Loos.

A Note on
the Transcription

Many so-called Great War diaries are actually reminiscences, maturer reflections of youthful action. Soldier-authors, long retired, in quiet leisure, have been able to revise their wartime logs to spit-and-polish perfection. Years, even decades later, these yellowed wartime diaries aid in the recollection of faded memories. To what degree such accounts have been "revised and expanded" is incalculable. The phraseology is smooth and polished, sentences and paragraphs orderly and structured.

This diary is not like that. It remains raw, uncorrected, and unpolished—straight from the tents and trenches where it was extemporaneously penned—much as Blake found Haig's diary.* I have retained where possible such ungrammatical constructions as run-on sentences, sentence fragments, and other constructions redolent of trench diary writing. In the interests of simple clarity and ease of reading I have capitalized words at the obvious beginning of sentences, lowercased others, and inserted occasional marks of punctuation to facilitate unlabored reading. Lionel habitually uses possessive apostrophes incorrectly, and I have taken the liberty of deleting them. I have corrected trivial errors in spelling, case, or tense only where the uncorrected text was unclear or misleading.

The precise meaning of certain turns of phrase has eluded me even after repeated study, but rather than excise all such phrases, I have decided to leave many of them as written to challenge readers to interpret them as they will. I have excised extraneous pedestrian passages, but of course have added nothing. In all my changes I have adhered to the most scrupulous caution in avoiding any altering of the meaning, emphasis, or nuance—thereby best preserving the sense of immediacy and authenticity of Lionel's words as found in the original handwritten diaries and letters.

---

* Robert Blake, *The Private Papers of Douglas Haig 1914–1919* (1952), preface, p. 11.

1 Crossing to France

30 December 1914–2 January 1915

DECEMBER 30 (WEDNESDAY) 10.30 P.M. News came I was to proceed with Captain Nicol, awful good sort and machine gunner, by earliest
morning train (about 2 A.M.) to Southampton. We decided we wouldn't do it.
5 months continual training—no holiday. So immensely bucked [up] we set
off from Sunderland 9.35 A.M.

~

DECEMBER 31 (THURSDAY) Last day of the old year. Eventually at
5 P.M. we reached Kings Cross. 1 hour late as our engine got rheumatism in an
axle and retired a casualty. Floods everywhere. By the way, we passed through
Ilford and I hear (now 1-1-15) that an awful smash-up of 70 casualties happened
next day there. Arrived London. Nicol went off to the Savoy & engaged rooms
for the night; I met Mr. Pemberton* at station & went to his new house where
I spent a happy 2½ hours. At 8 P.M. Nicol and I dined. 8.45 we proceeded to
the Alhambra and enjoyed ourselves. Saw many friends. About 1.30 A.M. we
returned to the Savoy & got up at 8 A.M. Wandered about and at last caught
the 9.25 train to Southampton on the 1st day of the New Year 1915 arriving ¾
hour late. We joined hands with an amusing fellow of the Gloucesters engaged
on the same errand. We found out the embarkation office, after passing armed
guards. An old buffer† asked us questions & gave us papers etc. We then were
told that we must leave Southampton by the 12 A.M. midnight packet boat to
Le Havre going out on the night of the first day of 1915. We then wandered in
the town, lunched at Old Sailors Hôtel and then purchased [gear]. It costs
more to go to the front than live 3 months in England. I thought I had
everything, but each shop suggested something more and last of all I bought
morphia, as it was told me 4 tablets would send me on the ebb-tide. 2 would

---

* Willoughby Pemberton, an old family friend.
† A Naval petty officer.

only be on the slack as I should come in again. The chemist was awful. He said if wounded I was to take 2 twice a day causing one to be unconscious for 24 hours (12 hours on stretch). He handed me a book with 50 in & then wanted me to buy chlorine or something, but I was fed up. We then went to hairdressers, where some stuff was offered & guaranteeing the hair not to grow any more for the time wished, and other love potions of similar quack notoriety. I left in disgust & went to buy some tickets at the Grand Theatre, "Count of Luxembourg." Asked for three, was given two—forgot to look, had to go back, and then we returned here to find I had lost them again. Some people take £100 to the front, but I am only taking £5 as I have no intention of accidentally enriching the German exchequer. I have already lost some of my equipment. 1 revolver pouch is missing, but that difficulty can be got over. Awful disaster I see railway smash at Ilford over 70 killed.* Also sister ship of Bulwark, great battleship gone down.† Possible submarine or mine. I suppose the papers will say as of yore "It is very unfortunate, but as it will have no material effect on the war we must look these things in the face, as they must happen." All very well, but when many ships go like this, What then, & we cross to-night. We had tea at 5 P.M.

Never have I seen such a gloomy lot of officers. The hotel is in the charge of embarkation buffers, about 200. Sentries guard each door. There are about 50 officers going out to-night, many Camerons & Black Watch. All have a gloomy expression, & we made awful jokes about them. An old fellow, a colonel, had had his hair shaven and his beard & looked a typical German, in fact I longed to arrest him. We called him Old Poodle, & looked quite annoyed. Oh, we must get off. Play quite good farce. What is to follow!

Today January 2nd 1915 we set sail in an awful wind. Instead of sailing at 12 midnight we started at 7 A.M. Nicol refused to get up. The sea I think. I went on deck and stayed there until we were clear, went down to breakfast where everyone was. Came on deck. A terrific sea was running, & we in going to Le

---

* A local Romford train, four minutes late, switched to the express track and into the path of a speeding Clacton-on-Sea express and they collided at 8:40 A.M. just on the London side of the Ilford Station. Both commuter trains were headed for the Liverpool Street Station in rush hour, New Year's Day being a normal business day in England at the time. Early reports gave 9 killed and 26 injured, but four days later the *Daily Mail* was reporting 10 deaths and 80 to 90 injured.

† The ship, the *Formidable,* a 15,000-ton pre-Dreadnought battleship laid down in 1901, was sunk by a German submarine, *U-24,* in the Channel near Plymouth, with a loss of 574. The *Formidable,* which gave its name to her class, was sister to the *Irresistible* and the *Implacable* as well as the *Bulwark,* which had been lost through accidental internal explosion in the Medway harbor on 26 November 1914.

Havre had it broad side on. I have never felt sea sick before, but I must confess I was not very well all the voyage. It was awful. After 2 hours everyone was spuing (sick), overboard, on the deck, in the cabins, in the smoke-room and corridors. Amid all this confusion I felt ill, but nothing more. I had to go on deck where the wind was colossal, & rain, sleet, & snow was falling. About 2.30 P.M. we landed & had to sign our names at the disembarkation office, left our luggage & boarded a Red waggon which conveyed us to L'Hôtel de Ville. Then we entered a room with the Brigadier & someone gave us tickets, next door we got our billeting tickets. We then took a fly to the commandant outside the town, and got orders from him. He said we were to proceed to our camp tomorrow. Remarked I was very young & I told him I was 22, and looks belied me.* To Negociant's Hôtel, 1 Rue Corneille our billet. Very pretty manageress & most entertaining. We then had tea, having had nothing since breakfast. After tea we took a walk. It was most embarrassing, as the people had never seen a kilt before & we were pestered. Nicol had not got his on as he is gun officer. We went into shops, & our French was appalling. Nothing but giggles came forth, & an audience collected. I wanted to get a waterproof cover for a match box, & having bought a French book with much trouble proceeded to look up waterproof. However it was not there. So at a huge millinery establishment I proceeded to tell about a dozen serving ladies my wishes. At length the suggestion "preventez l'eau dans la boix [boîte]" caught on & they saw my wish. Said, I believe, they had none in stock but farther up, etc. We then returned. Had dinner. Afterwards I took a walk through the streets & got to bed about 2 A.M. Quite pleased with Le Havre.

---

* Lionel was just twenty at the time.

2 With the Black Watch at Le Havre

3–27 January 1915

JANUARY 3 (SUNDAY) Slept well. At 9 A.M. someone came in and shouted something about déjeuner, the breakfast I suppose which he brought me. I then proceeded to dress & by 11 A.M. was ready for Church. Nicol wouldn't come, & Scott was reluctant, but at last he consented. We went rather hazy. Having no books, no French, & believing the French were Catholics. However we set out & arrived at the Promenade & walked about. Time went very quickly, & we came back at 1 P.M. for another déjeuner they called. This time the hotel is full of ladies & other things. I said "avez-vous papier pour écrire" and got some writing paper, wonderful. Better French than last night when I wanted some waterproof covering for a match box and mixed up German & French and said "préventez l'eau zu kommen" prevent water to come in. We are off to the camp or somewhere at 3 P.M.

There are about 35 officers in this camp, 1 major, 2 captains, & myself being in the Black Watch, also Gloucesters, Camerons, Munsters, S.W. Borders [South Wales Borderers] & Welsh regiments, or rather portions & drafts.* We hear they only entered into this camp yesterday having come from another which was condemned, so the story runs, because 2 men disappeared in the mud & were lost as well as a horse & cart. This is bad enough but I am thoroughly enjoying life, [even though] this may sound pessimistic in parts. Apparently I may go up country any day.

Awful rain today! Mud ghastly. A river is flowing through my tent which is on the side of a hill. Have to get a new servant, my man has succumbed to life out

---

* A draft was a group of soldiers that had arrived in France but had not yet been assigned to a particular unit.

here. This place is dreary. Rain all day. Havre always the same. No work. I am getting to work on alterations in my tent. 6 P.M. dinner, then to bed.

~

JANUARY 6 (WEDNESDAY) What an awful night. Such rain I've never known. All went well till somewhere in the night—what time I don't know—but suddenly a hurricane got up & rain awful splashed down. My poor old tent was not proof against it, & after much throbbing collapsed. I had no bed companion, so had to fend for myself. I felt at first I was going to be suffocated but after ages, time I do not know, I got hold of my skindle [knife] which was very sharp & hacked a hole through. Having emerged I was sopped with rain. I am rather gratified to see I am not the only sufferer, several other tents are down & others show signs. Feeling hopelessly bored I wandered to tin hut, where troops are going later, & collecting some goods, slept on & off fitfully to morning. 3 other fellows joined me. I think we all were pervaded with shivers, because in the morning at daylight we were sorry spectacles, sopping wet, no chance [to dry out] today & all goods soaked. I spent all morning rescuing belongings & getting another tent, which looks much more serviceable.

A subaltern of the Sussex, whose name continually slips me, seeing the good qualities of the tent joins me. He's a good fellow. My spirits rose with day, & in the afternoon I determined to go to town to get dry. I set out with Gray of the Cameronians who is also a thoroughly good fellow. On the way in the train we met a fellow of the Seaforths who knew several of our fellows. He had returned from the front & showed me his hand. Had lost a finger. Awful sight, but a better wound than some I suppose. He said the Black Watch, Camerons & Gordons were awfully unlucky in this war & had had awful losses, indeed Black Watch had lost 2,100 already & over 60 officers. He also said it was as good as signing your death warrant to join them, as they were practically in all the worst fighting, & were always used for reinforcements. However nothing is going to deter me. I've never felt so happy in my life, & don't mind how long I stay out in France.

~

JANUARY 7 (THURSDAY) Pouring rain. Very good tent. The water only runs with gurgles underneath the boards—sends one to sleep. One gets used to damp things, & indeed expecting nothing else one feels the same as usual. Rain all afternoon. There are about 80 officers here now, & almost 7,000 troops, all drafts. We heard heavy firing at about 3 P.M. where we didn't know, but it seemed close. Some one said it was at a German aeroplane. Several have

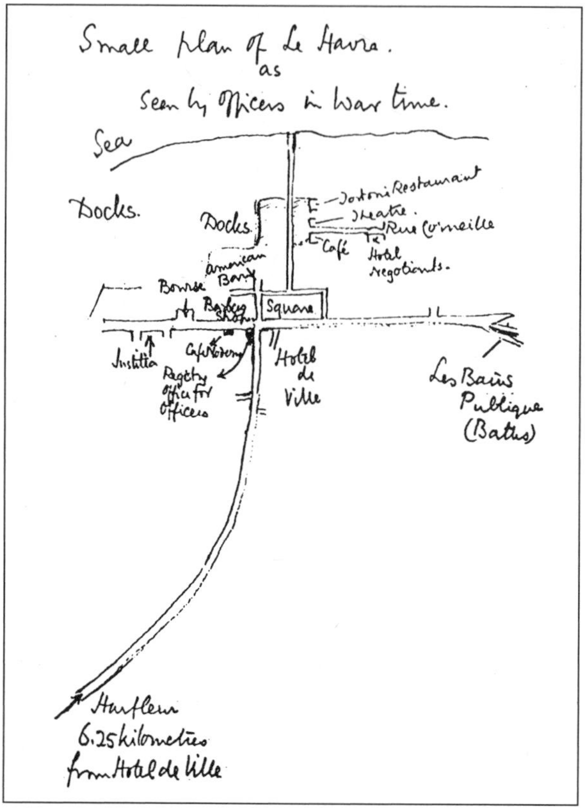

Map 1. Lionel's hand-drawn map of Le Havre.

been seen here & they fear they will attack this camp with Bombs. If so, they will slaughter hundreds. Rain all day. I spent the afternoon censoring letters for my men and other people. A chap has just come in to say that two Tommies being bored with life started shooting one another; about eight shots were fired, & at last one got it in the neck or somewhere, & now is a corpse. He says someone will be needed to attend the funeral tomorrow. That's usually the case, for a fellow had to take a party today for that purpose. The reason for death I do not know.

This quite an exciting spot as things are bound to happen. Forgot to say we saw a train full of broken rifles (butts broken off, muzzles twisted & broken, awful sights) go by today. Our camp is by the side of the railway & everything from the front passes by us. At about 3 P.M. 400 men streamed into the camp, some without boots, caps, stockings indeed a piteous spectacle. These were all refitted out. They were fighting last night, so they said. Such filthy creatures I've never seen before. I suppose I shall be one in a few days.

JANUARY 8 (FRIDAY) We keep usual time. Cannot stop praising my tent, it is splendid. At about 10 A.M. a quantity of aeroplanes were discerned very high up, looking like birds. There must have been at least 10 & they had the appearance of being chased by each other but I don't know, they were too high up.

At 1.30 P.M. I decided to spend the afternoon in Havre. Then we set out for a bath. We learnt that <u>Les baines publique</u> were situated in the Rue Strassbourg. We found them and enjoyed a lovely bath, the best I have had for 5 months. The most notable thing that struck me was the soap. It was of a pink colour & smelt of lavender, but was of the most exquisite nature totally unlike most soaps. I shall never forget its good qualities. Of course I could not speak enough French to find out its chemical properties, so the opportunity slipped by. On emerging into the street, despite the pouring rain & sleet, we felt quite happy & content with the world. Such was the effect of the warm baths. I then started purchasing articles most needed. Really I do not know what I shall do if I stay here much longer, for I find every day there is something more I need. Thus my valise* is visibly growing in size, & by the time I reach the actual trenches I shall be a merchandise seller in reality. At length at 4.30 P.M. I reached Transatlantique postal depot & enquired if any letters had come for me. They said no.

At 5.30 P.M. I left & returned Tortoni's for dinner. I met some of our fellows & had the usual dinner of oysters, soup, omelette, cutlet, pineapple & dessert. As I had had no breakfast & no lunch & no tea I was slightly hungry & we enjoyed ourselves. We left 7 P.M. my friends going elsewhere but where I did not enquire. I boarded a Harfleur train at 7.30 P.M. & had a most interesting talk with some Tommies back from the front. I think they said they were the Munsters, but am not sure. They were from the same division as the Argyll & Sutherlands. The stories they had to tell were most interesting & extremely hard to set down on paper. All 6 declared themselves fed up with the war, much to my surprise. They said they had been in the firing line for 2 months & were now back in Havre for a rest cure which they said consisted of 12 hours fatigue duties every day. They said it was no rest & they were worn out & would return to the front in a few days. I must confess feeling sorry for them; for not returning to a proper rest after being in the thick of it for 2 months & other people getting rest is certainly a hard lot to bear. I explained that in wartime many small things passed unnoticed & that they were merely unlucky as some

---

* An elongated duffel bag.

small mistake had probably been made on paper. They were Regulars & I have met many others who have been back to England for a rest after only 6 weeks of fighting, but after all everyone cannot be treated the same. One of them told me that he had been in the same trench as the Argylls & he pities the sufferings of some as awful. Not enough clothes & frozen cold. He said he saw 6 of them one day lying down motionless, & a doctor coming pronounced it as strangulation of the blood, in other words they had been frozen to death in the early hours of the morning. The same narrator said that he had looted the clothes from some of the dead, and feeling a compassion for the kilted ones had given them some to put on. He also went on to say that the brogue shoes worn by the Highlanders were useless in the trenches as the mud in places reached to the knees, & one was stuck in the slime. After a few hours of this suffering the men would try to disengage their limbs from the unwilling embrace & in so doing left their shoes and sometimes their stockings thickly adhered to the mud. Now stocking-less and boot-less their plight was miserable, & their bare legs rapidly got frostbitten. He said that at this stage there were more casualties of frostbitten feet than of actually wounded. Another of the Tommies gave me another thrilling experience. He said that he and some others were in a particularly bad part of the trenches, & the mud was frightful in fact they sank so far as to make their heads, when standing upright, quite invisible from the enemy, & a few inches from the top of the trenches. Quite useless for firing as they could not even look over. He said they suffered like this for 24 hours at least, without food or water as a particularly heavy fire was going on & no one could approach. The Germans got to hear of their plight and charge[d]. Result, the men never heard them coming & being nearly up to their waists in mud & quite incapable of moving, were ruthlessly bayonetted. They were totally unable to reply, & he said that at least a hundred must have thus perished. He and several others feigned death & so escaped as very shortly afterwards the British charged, seeing that only a portion of their trench in front had been captured, & as there were only a hundred or so Germans in possession they in turn were slaughtered, being more or less in the same plight. The Tommy in question thus escaped with nothing worse than a few bruises caused by a falling rifle. They all complained that about 200 men were buried to the rear of their trench one day, with only a few inches of soil above them. It was alright at first, but then the wind shifted & the decaying & pestilential bodies wafted their od[or]iferous perfumes into their trenches. They described this as the worst experience of all. That night they lodged a complaint & the bodies were covered with some substance, lime, they said, which stopped the inconvenience. They were full of experiences, most interesting to hear, & the authenticity I can hardly doubt. Unfortunately the train reached Harfleur and I had to depart. I then descended & started on my muddy walk back to the camp. I eventually got to bed about 9 P.M. I found another fellow in our tent, a friend of Dickers, who was an old campaigner, looks a good sort, but will be off soon I think.

~

JANUARY 9 (SATURDAY) As the tent leaked slightly during the night I got up earlier than usual, at 9.30 that is to say. It is a curious fact how one exists on such little food here. I manage to go without breakfast or luncheon & then go to Le Havre in the afternoon at 1.30 P.M. have a cup of chocolate, & then a really good dinner at 7 P.M. Perhaps we can attribute it to a total absence of work, the awful rain & muddy conditions. Anyway I am quite content, as to pay the awful Jew, who cheats us at the mess 3 francs a day, for the bread meals & chicory which we get, is a farce. I set off with Dicker & Austin to the town. We went next to the Negociant's Hôtel to call for letters in case some had come for me. We made up the following sentence with only one mistake that I can see, that "ont" for "sont." "Est[-]ce que des lettres pour moi sont arrivées?" It worked, but no letters came. An interpreter persisted in looking at our <u>reschau</u> [*réchaud,* portable stove], said we could get a much better one, "un reschau du soldat" which is really consolidated paraffin. Better than running stuff as you can carry plenty, & is obtainable when the other is not. So we took our <u>reschau</u> back and said "changes." They were unwilling and started off an awful face. They spoke of the "reschau du soldat" and said deux heures & dix heures. We thought they meant we were to come back in 2 hours. So we started off. Apparently the chap meant the small tins would last 2 hours & the large ones ten hours. He handed us back & we completed the purchase. There is something indescribably funny in buying things in France as I am sure they try to cheat you. Take this instance. We were in the Café Moderne & asked for 3 chocolats (drinks). When I said <u>"l'addition"</u> i.e. the bill, the waiter, a foolish & comic fellow, said "cinq francs." He persisted, we told him to go to several places at once and then demanded the price of each individual chocolat (70 centimes) making 2 francs 10 centimes. We caught him out & said several things as well. These people really are rotten. They don't help their visitors at all, but this of course only refers to a few of the low class.

Coming back that night I never laughed so much in all my life. We had had a good dinner at Tortoni's & were in good spirits. We boarded the last train (8.15 P.M.) to Harfleur. It was a one-coach affair for a wonder not nearly big enough. We got on alright. At the Place de l'Hôtel de Ville crowds tried to get in. No use. A burly policeman got on however. The conductor was useless & could not get anyone to pay. We retreated inside a little. At length Tommies climbed in to every conceivable place, some were half on the roof, others on the step & some hanging on behind. The language was awful. The policeman was impotent with rage. At last he was nearly lifted off his feet and shoved off the train. Everybody roared. The conductor yelled for his fares. So he stopped the train. However, someone else tugged the bell, so on we went again. This happened every few minutes, whenever the conductor got an arm free. Thus we stopped every hundred yards or so. Meanwhile the Tommies at the back, a little the worse for liquor, shouted "Tottenham Court Road—All change—Oxford Circus" & other balderdash indescribably funny at the time, but impossible to put on paper. We gradually moved on, 1 man inside began to sing Tipperarie. There was an old French man inside with a very furious face & he evidently had a headache. He got purple with anger, & I believed demanded the ejection of the individual. Nobody was keen on the job, & as he was not going to do it himself the noise went on. At last he was fed up & told the conductor, I believe, to force a path. So the conductor led the way to the exit, & he followed. Some Tommies then pushed them both overboard & rang the bell. Off we went at a great pace, without a conductor. We went two miles without stopping, as there being no conductor, & we not having reached our destination the bell was never pulled for people to get on. The scene was awfully funny. At length we disembarked & returned to camp. It was impossible for us to have done anything, as to say anything to half drunk soldiers leads to a row, a thing we are warned against.

∽

JANUARY 10 (SUNDAY) Le Havre on Sunday in wartime is quite different to Le Havre on any week day. Everyone seems to be out of doors, whether it rains or not & today it poured all day showed what the people are made of. We wandered in as usual in the afternoon and enjoyed ourselves as in the preceding days. The following is a small summary of Le Havre, as seen by any officer remaining a few days at the base.

Le Havre itself is situated at the entrance to the River Seine, on the left bank going upstream. The city does not stretch inland, but is very narrow, being constructed along the banks. The docks enter the heart of the town, the chief of which is the Bassin de l'ever [levé?]. On the right side of this dock is now situated the Transatlantique postal depot. That is where all parcels, after being passed by the censor, go to. Letters from England for the troops also pass through this place. It is purely military. The Hôtel de Ville can be taken as the centre of the town & from it radiate in all directions the trains. Practically opposite is a large building, where we, as officers, have to go to register themselves after giving in their names at the disembarkation office at the quay. Between the Hôtel de Ville & this building runs the longest street in the town. It starts from the jetty & stretches to Harfleur practically straight the whole way. At right angles to this road is the Rue Strassbourg, the finest street of all. On the left hand side, after coming out of the Hôtel de Ville one comes to the Café Moderne, which is the chief assembly ground. Further on is the Justitia, quite a fine building. The street turning to the left before coming to it must ever remain well known to officers who have been to pay their men for on the left hand side, 20 yards away is the building for drawing pay for the drafts. The method of procedure is most irritating, as sometimes you are kept waiting 2 hours. Almost opposite the Justitia in the same street is the Bourse, in an upper room of which lives the "Censor." By continuing to the end of the street, & turning to the left you find yourself in the promenade facing the other bank of the Seine & half faces the sea. To return, by proceeding along the main street by the Hôtel de Ville, you come to the large square, with a bandstand. On the left hand side is a Barber's shop that most must frequent. Further on the left is the American bar, a favourite resort of some. By continuing by the side of the train lines & turning the corner you pass on the left one of the biggest shops in the town, the one where I got my "reschau du soldat." Further on you reach a large square. On the left are the docks, on the right are 3 separate buildings, the theatre in the centre, a café on the right, & the Tortoni Restaurant on the left. Passing down a street in the Rue Corneille one sees on the left, the Negociant's Hôtel where I was billeted the first night in Havre. The only other place of importance is "Les Bains Publique," which is situated in Strassbourg Street, and very nice too. These are the chief things which we see in wartime, but [what] there is in Peacetime when the casino is open (now used for the wounded) I do not know. But it is a very dull place at present, as no theatres are open at all.

～

JANUARY 11 (MONDAY) I had to get up at 6.30 A.M. to take a party to dig trenches on a hill. A more amusing and uncomfortable time I've never known—uncomfortable because of the pouring rain, amusing because of the men's method of keeping up their spirits. We started work at 7.30 Although only 1 mile away you cannot walk direct because you would be promptly submerged in water up to the neck. As I say we started work at 7.30 Digging commenced after a quarter of an hour, the rain started and the men resented it, 6 shovels were placed deeply in the ground & owing to the weight, when heaving up, snapped in two. Having no more implements I sent them back to bring some more spades. I never saw those men for the rest of the day as they were evidently fed up. The men not being of my regiment, & totally unknown to me, I didn't much care. Soon I heard a splash & yells. One man had tapped a water pipe. Why it was up there I don't know but it was, & the man was down in the hole wet through. Some fellows went to relieve him, as did several others, but they were too anxious to help, & sent several more of their number sprawling down. Indeed I saw some revelling in it, shoving and hitting others from behind. I called them off and gave them a sharp lecture. They were quiet then. At 12 I went for some biscuits, while they had some lunch up there. All these men were back from the front after two months fighting & were supposed to be having their rest cure, but this consisted in 12 hours fatigue each day. I am really sorry for them as they are going to the front again shortly. They have been overlooked I suppose. On coming back at 1 P.M. I found the trench they were engaged upon overflowing with water. We spent 3 hours in draining the water off, & then thoroughly fed up, we departed. Having dug a trench 50 yards long, & 3 feet deep in about 9 hours with 100 men. This works out per man, very few spadefuls I should think. But as there seemed little object in the work no one had much heart in it; I was not surprised. The rain was awful [to]day so I was glad when the day came to an end at last.

~

JANUARY 12 (TUESDAY) I had to take 100 men down to Le Havre to unload a train which had just come in from the front. It consisted of broken rifles, smashed guns, blood-stained coats & kits of every description. A more gruesome work could hardly be imagined. All these things had just arrived from the front, not many miles away. Some of the rifles had their barrels smashed in half, others again had them twisted right round, in the most peculiar shapes. Some had the stocks blown off, others were merely cut and scratched with pieces of shrapnel I should suppose. Many rifles were still loaded , but could not go off because they either had no barrel, or no cocking piece, to let the striker fly forward. Some of the fellows disliked the work of pulling the coats & things out, because they were all messy, but towards the end of the day the dirty work was done & everything piled up at the side. One of the most peculiar things was that of a small cannon, which had its muzzle locked up with a piece of shell fired by the enemy. This seemed the only injury, though of course the mechanism may have been affected. It poured all day & we were soaked through when we knocked off at 4 P.M. I've never known such weather, it's hardly stopped raining since I came to this place, much worse than in England, indeed England's not in the running. Luckily our camp is on a hill, so we do not feel the situation so badly as if we were in a valley at the bottom.

I was speaking to Jener, Austin's servant this morning, & the more one hears the more one realizes the little the public in England really know about the war. He is in the Royal Sussex Regiment, & the Regular Battalion not being up to strength, several Special Reservists were drafted into it. Accordingly he went abroad in the first week of the war and gave me a few facts to think about this morning. He said that about the first bit of fighting his Brigade encountered was just before the Retreat. His regiment was the advance guard, & they were going along a very dusty straight road without seeing so much as a scout. Suddenly having passed 2 hay stacks they got [it] in the neck. Enemy in great force was advancing & their losses were awful. Retreat is not the right word he said; it was a rout. The Sussex were now the rear guard & suffered most of the attack. So furious was the hurry that they threw away haversacks & great coats & the people in front shouted out to go slower but they hurried on. At length they went through a village & no sooner than the last company had gone through than 5 minutes later the place was shelled, the Germans having the range beforehand. After that the rout went on & the losses were awful, until reinforcements came & the tidal wave receded, but it was no retreat in parts, it was a rout & nothing else & it speaks extraordinarily well for our commanders to have received so comparatively few losses, to what may have been possible.

∽

JANUARY 13 (WEDNESDAY) Awful gale in the night, we thought the tent was coming down but it held up alright. An awful draught blew through the whole night. I had a cold in the morning, so lay in bed for a little. I soon got up. By the way two others of the Second Black Watch came in yesterday one being a full lieutenant. At 9.30 A.M. Captain Davy came in and told me I was to be Orderly Officer for the day, as Richard of the Black Watch, who was the detailed one, was off to the front.* As Orderly Officer I have to be in camp all day, doing various duties by the night. They are enumerated below:—

Duties of Orderly Officer—No. 1 Infantry Base Depot.
I took over the duties of orderly officer at Reveille, 6.30 A.M. (which I didn't) and the orderly sergeant reported at 7 P.M. the previous evening (which he didn't)

---

* Lt. John Ernest Richard, also attached to the Black Watch from the Argyll and Sutherland Highlanders, joined a group of more experienced officers sent to train the drafts passing through the 3rd (Special Reserve) Battalion at Etaples. The 3rd Battalion never saw action in France, serving primarily as a training ground for drafts to the other fighting battalions.

I visited the dinners at 12.45 P.M. and the second sitting at 1.15 P.M. and found all correct.

I visited the cook house at 12.30 P.M. and found them cleaned up.

I visited the Quarter Guard 11.30 A.M. by day and at 1.30 A.M. by night. I found the sentries alert and acquainted into their duties.

I visited the Canteen at 12 noon when I opened it, also at 3 P.M. and 8 P.M. at which hours I found it closed.

I visited the Sergeants mess 2 P.M. and found everything in order.

I visited the Garrison Guard twice by day at 10 A.M. & 6 P.M. and once by night at 11.30 P.M. and found the sentries acquainted into their orders.

(signed) R.M.M.Davy, Capt & Adjutant

No. 1 Infantry Base Depot

The Garrison Guard consisted of sentries stationed outside the camp & also guarding the railway below. The Quarter Guard consisted of a guard & sentries posted inside the camp, guarding the road & cook houses. All duties were successfully carried out, & the only amusing report was that of a sentry on the Garrison Guard. He reported that at about 11 P.M. at night he saw something approaching very slowly & imagined it was a spy, he fired one shot. After challenging three times hit the object & found it was a huge cat, which he showed me. Indeed its size was colossal being at least 4 feet long.* I believe it was subsequently buried. The only other thing was opening the canteen at 12 noon, because the orderly officer is supposed to taste the beer & announce if it is good or not. I dislike beer intensely, & so told one of the privates in there to taste it, which he thereupon did, drinking practically two pints out of a jug before we could stop him, & then it was only because he was out of breath. That satisfied us the beer was alright. The sellers of the beer were bored because they said he should only have sipped it; the private immensely furious, said that he could not taste beer until he had drunk 3 or 4 pints, & said he was trying to do them a good turn by saying the beer was good when he had not sufficiently tested. Having had enough of the squabble, I declared the beer good & decamped with the Battalion orderly sergeant, who normally accompanies one of these visits.

Very wet all day. We heard a great deal of heavy firing at about 12 noon and also at about 5 P.M. it seemed to come from the N East & as the wind was blowing from that direction it may have been further off than we thought.

---

* Lionel is no doubt overly enthusiastic in his estimate.

By the number of officers & men coming out here I should think we are considering some big advance other than trench work, over 30,000 men & 70 officers came in yesterday & they come up every day. I am beginning to consider what is the matter in England. Have not received a letter the whole time I have been out here which is just about 2 weeks. Has anything gone wrong? I must have written about 10. I received a parcel from Oldham the day before yesterday containing some meat lozenges, soap, & shaving stuff. Also last night 3 blankets arrived from Caley's. These are most acceptable, as up till now I have slept in my valise, with only a fleabag to give warmth. A <u>Fleabag</u> is a bag 6 feet long (or thereabouts) made of a blanket of 3 thicknesses, you get into it, as the sides are sewn up, & either sleep with 2 thicknesses above you & 1 under you, or with 1 above & 2 under. The differences are in former, more warmth & a hard surface to lie on, & in the latter less warmth. I completed my orderly officer's job at 1.30 midnight & handed it in at 9.30 A.M. next morning.

～

JANUARY 14 (THURSDAY) Woke up 8.30 A.M. was told I was to take command of the 1st Battalion Black Watch draft, which had come in under the command of Lt. Davey of the Cameron Highlanders. On proceeding to the orderly room & handing in my orderly officer Report, I was told to equip the draft but that only 90 were to be equipped with the sheepskin coats & vests. I thereupon proceeded to do so. I found that 7 had proceeded to the Y.M.C.A. rooms. These I severely admonished for being absent when called upon as I had previously ordered everyone to be in the lines ready to move off at ½ an hour's notice, as was written on the order. No sooner were the men equipped with the goat skin (not sheep) coats, than they hastily donned them & behaved ridiculously. The coats or jackets in question I should say are about 4½ feet long and are covered with long fur about 6" [of the] stuff. The consequence was that the men looked like a lot of sheep or goats or bears & to denote the change started to bah after the manner of sheep. At length this species of amusement seemed to tire them & [they] started to play about with them until [they were] stopped. The ordinary Tommie is a most extraordinary fellow, & it needs a great deal of time in studying him to give anything like an accurate description of his qualities, defects & their opposites. It can be said, however, with absolute truth that he is the most wonderful, the enduring & the most devil may care human being in existence. This does I think sum him up in a few words. He grouses as all true soldiers do, if he did not grouse, then he could not be a true Tommy. If you give him one thing, he wants another, it is not really that he wants or needs it, but it is outcome of usually idleness, or nothing to do; it merely means that he wants to get on to a brisker business & get going, which two things are closely allied; proving I think that idleness, or a life without any real excitement, is his greatest enemy, & can only be fought by grousing, which is a valve or safety exit. I have heard many officers say that what the Tommies go through at the front is truly wonderful. They grouse but that is all. Their perseverance is dogged & seems to have no limit. Many instances have been given, where we, having been relieved by the French or Indians have found those trenches lost in the morning because the endurance of these men was not up to ours. No. Our fellows will go through anything, & they deserve the greatest praise. Of course there are exceptions, indeed quite a few, but are there not in everything, & does not "the exception prove the rule," as the saying is. Unfortunate to say, I have heard cases in this Camp, where men have been known to persistently desert; they have been sent with a draft, feigned sickness, got sent back, ordered off again, & then found to be absent from Roll call, & to miss several successive drafts by absenting themselves. These men are no good & are cowards. There must be some in every nation. Luckily there are few. This is the worst type. There is one other; the man in the firing line who gets fed up with cold & exposure, wants to get back; he, to obtain this object either holds up a hand or a leg, & keeps it there until he is hit. Thereupon he yells aloud that he's wounded & gets carried off by the ambulance next night. There are others who purposely inflict rifle wounds on themselves. I have been told this by many officers & sergeants back from the front, & so it unfortunately must be authentic, much as it is deplorable. These men can hardly be classed among the shirkers & deserters, because it must, undeniably, need some courage to expose yourself unnecessarily & wait until you get shot or on the other hand to inflict a wound upon yourself. Thus these men are not as bad but of little use to their country, if they so behave; given an advance & none of this trench warfare, better fighters or soldiers could not be found, so that it is extremely unfair to class them with the other material [the shirkers and deserters]. There can be no doubt that it needs & calls for exceptional endurance and fortitude to live through 36 hours & sometimes many days in a trench with mud to your knees, a drenching rain, perhaps a sharp frost, & little or no food, when there is exceptional vigilance on the enemy's part against relief & food supplies coming up. So people in England, if they hear of these people, should not condemn them without giving them a hearing as all people are not blessed with the same endurance & vitality.

I have seen some of Kitchener's army & a fine lot they look, some have already proved themselves worthy to be regulars. To look at them one cannot help noticing the difference. They are fine strapping fellows, many 6 feet high & into a better appearance than the ordinary Tommie mainly due I suppose because they come from a different sphere of life, with perhaps much money, & have led clean lives & what is more have passed a pretty high standard of fitness. How a battalion of these fellows will shape remains to be seen.

What has the remainder of the day in store for me? It is now 11.30 A.M. Had also the same morning to attend trial of a corporal of the Black Watch, who seemed to have been absent for 5 days when on a journey to Boulogne. I asked the Adjutant if I could rush down & get pay for my men of the (details) of the Black Watch. He said yes so I scooted. Only details get payed here, drafts do not. Details consist of men coming in from hospital or back from the firing line for a rest. There are about 20 in the 1st Battalion & 40 in 2nd Battalion of the Black Watch. I paraded my draft for the C.O.'s [Commanding Officer's] inspection. Colonel Kidwood inspected & gave me various documents to read to the men. I did so. We are off to-morrow I think. Sergeant Munro of the Black Watch, going home for an operation, gave me a souvenir I shall always keep & is a slip of paper wherein is inscribed

Gift from

Mary R
and the

women of the empire

1914

He assured me he had another one. He also said only a certain number had gone out so that they were unique. I am keeping it & shall never let it go.

〜

JANUARY 15 (FRIDAY) I inspected my draft & saw all men were present. At 10.30 A.M. the adjutant told me that Gracey was taking it up to the front but was only conducting it there. So I am not to go into the trenches yet. I am absolutely fed up, as I was expecting to go up with it, & I loathe this life here. I suppose they are keeping me back to join the 2nd Battalion, which is refitting a little way back from the firing line. They left the trenches on Xmas eve for 1 month's rest, so it is due to go up next week. I have been longer at this place than anyone else, and it does not please me, except that I suppose I shall be seeing if some officers come up again who have already gone up, because they say the average life of an officer at the front is a week or so before he gets wounded or sent back.

JANUARY 16 (SATURDAY) Have caught a chill, as there was awful rain in the night about 11 P.M. Such a deluge as I should have enjoyed seeing in daylight in good shelter, but at night it was awful. I woke up hearing an awful rainstorm. The hail was coming down so heavy that I thought it would come through the tent. This continued for about ½ an hour with intermittent thunder. Suddenly I felt myself growing very cold underneath, so I shifted about & tried to get to sleep. At length I felt cold all over & really damp, so I stretched out for my electric torch on a box by my side, & accidentally knocked it over, it fell into some water with a splash. I eventually found it and flashed it on. What was my horror to see the tent with water about 3 inches deep & various articles floating about. The water was by now steadily flowing into my valise, & as little comfort could be derived by staying in bed, I got up thoroughly cold & damp. I splashed about & [in] vain tried to find the door; this after much trouble I found, and undid the strings; I got out. The awful rain & hail still continued, and I endeavoured to find the reason for my inundation. I found it. The tents are on the side of a hill, & the consequence is that one side has to be hewn out of the earth, while the other has to be raised in order to form a small plateau for the tent. Apparently earth had fallen in on both sides & prevented the water running away very quickly. Thus it filled the tent first & had to run over the boards. Exit was then very difficult, as the water had to soak underneath the canvas to get out, thus the interior of the tent formed a bath. With my hands I hauled away at the earth & eventually got rid of the water, but it left the bottom of the tent covered with mud, as also my valise & all my articles. I was soaked, having nothing on except my pajamas, in which attire I had gone out to battle with the elements. I saw no sleep would be possible that night so I hunted about for my candles & found 6 which had floated down the tent & had come to rest on my glengarry (Highland cap). These I eventually lit with some matches, providence had told me to keep in my rucksack, which I always kept hung up on the tent pole. The candles spluttered but at length lit up. I then unearthed my "reschau du soldats" & got all 4 of them burning. Things then looked more cheerful, as the heat given out by these objects was quite considerable. I then got out my Burberry & put it on although it was wet, but it could not have been wetter than anything else, so therein I found consolation. I then set to work to examine my valise. This I found full of water & I emptied it outside as by now the rain was over. I returned to the tent & sorted various articles. I suddenly noticed that the tent was beginning to get quite light so I looked out & noticed that the clouds had all gone & it was starlight, with a small bit of moon on the horizon. I got all my belongings outside & shook the water out. At about 1 A.M. so my watch told me (luckily it had not played me false & stopped) it began to freeze, so I took all my belongings in & tried to dry them. By now the 4 spirit stoves & 4 candles had raised the temperature to about 100° Fahrenheit, but there was one disadvantage, steam started to rise from the sodden blankets & clothes until the place was like a Turkish Bath. As the heat was unbearable, being of a moist nature, I had perforce to put the stoves out & thought that I would seek sleep. One waterproof sheet looked fairly dry, so I rolled myself up in it & sought sleep. About 3 A.M. I woke up frozen to death & shivering. I lighted all the stoves & candles & looked outside. Hard frost & ground crisp, so went inside again & lit my pipe, sitting on an old box, as the valise & blanket were unbearable. I then extinguished 3 stoves & kept one going. I remained like this till daybreak sitting on an old box with a small stove in front. It was fairly light at 7 A.M. so I got up & hauled all my belongings out. These dried fairly quickly as a breeze blew, but my kilt is still damp as its thickness does not allow of quick drying. I dressed myself in a wet shirt & damp clothes & walked about. I then found I had to take a party of 200 men to put up tents. I was occupied at this job from 8 A.M. till 4.30 P.M. I was damp & cold all day & felt rotten. Upon returning to my tent I found things still damp but better. All 4 stoves were giving forth colossal heat & drying out the place. At about 6 P.M. these stoves had consumed all their methylated spirits & having performed their duty were of no more use. They cost 2 francs 5 centimes each & last about 15 hours continuously. As I felt very tired & had eaten nothing hardly all day, I retired to rest about 7 P.M.

❧

JANUARY 17 (SUNDAY) A wasted night. Very little sleep & horrible shivers. I hope to goodness I shall not fall sick & get invalided back, as that would be too awful. I got up at 8 A.M. from a damp bed and proceeded to have breakfast. It was a farce, I was not hungry and could not eat, also a head[ache] was coming on. At 10 A.M. the Adjutant sent for me & told me that a draft of the Black Watch was coming in (110 men) & that I was to go to the trenches with them later on. I received various orders concerning them, chief of which was this, which I will write down as it may be of interest in days to come.

To be read on 3 successive Parades:
Loss of Kit: O.C. [Officer Commanding] units will take every means to stop their men losing or selling their kits. It should be pointed out that at this stage of the war, when it is difficult to get sufficient clothing, this conduct is playing into the hands of the enemy. Once a kit is completed and a man is found

deficient of anything, he will be severely punished. If necessary a Kit Inspection should be held daily of those men likely to lose their kit.

I certify this was read out on three successive parades.

Date_____   Commanding 2nd Battalion

Thus a draft of the regiment & battalion to which I have been attached for the duration of the war is at last coming. I am also orderly officer today and have to go through the same duties as last time. Have still got an awful headache. Will try some quinine. It is very odd, I see that 8 drafts are coming to-day each in charge of an officer, all these officers after reporting to the O.C. reinforcements are to return back to England & are not to proceed to the front, and we are here taking them up country. As there are only 9 of us here now 1 will be left behind, which looks very much like as if they are cleaning this depot out for a new army to come out, perhaps a division of Kitchener's army. It seems to me that it is the last wag of the regular army because the 28th Division landed yesterday & has ever since been making its way up country. Some of K's army are I believe coming out this month so that our army out here must have grown to a great size by now. Probably we shall try a strong attack shortly, who knows. Kitchener is not sending such quantities over for nothing & a general advance seems likely.

How mad people must be in England not to have conscription, nothing but that can possibly defeat Germany. It is no good getting troops by the voluntary system, as although they may be a better class, you will never get enough. Germany can easily raise enough to counteract the number. We must have a huge army of many millions, and the sooner it is raised and equipped the sooner the war will be over. We are not fighting an ordinary nation, we are fighting a nation of the most wonderful organization & discipline as has ever existed & ever will exist. It is a mistake to believe we can crush Germany as we are at present. When I was in Germany from January 10th to July 19th 1914 last year I saw what a perfect nation they are in some ways. They will fight to the last, but in my opinion, if we go on as at present, there will be no last for are not the enemy in everybody else's country, except for a small piece of Alsatia? They are looking from their point of view in a better position than anyone else, but from ours, and a rather narrow one at that, in the case of some people, it would seem they have their back broken, & are being smashed up. It is all very well for the papers to hide certain facts in order not to cause a panic, but why not own up to some things instead of slurring them over? Come up and say "Yes, the Russians did meet defeat at Lodz & other places. The Germans won there & people who do not acknowledge an enemy's fine performance, are not sportsmen." I admire it. For a nation which can tackle England, France, Belgium & Russia at the same time, & then carry the fight into their foe's country is a nation to respect, & to admire its victories even at our own expense. Some people say this is pro-German. Well, I prefer not to be narrow-minded, but to take into consideration other people's assets, & whether England wins or not, I shall always admire Germany for what she is. The Personification of organization & zeal, though her zeal may lead her astray sometimes. As things go at present, I think we shall be lucky to drive the Germans back into their country & then declare peace, for, a person who has never been in Germany before, little understands a German's spirit, & the nation's fortifications.

Really I think that today I have heard the most lugubrious talk in all my life. In speaking to the Battalion orderly sergeant while waiting for the men's dinners to be served he said that he thought peace would be declared very soon, as all the men at the front were sick of the war, & everyone was crying out for peace. I just told him off by sections, so to speak. He seemed quite flabbergasted when I told him how eager everyone was to get out. He agreed after some time, but brightened up when he thought he had a depressing argument to tell me. He said "Yes! They may be eager in England, but two weeks of work at the front made them sick of it, & they wanted peace at once." This sort of man is dangerous as he is apt to infect others with his unpatriotic & silly ideas, so I found a delight in telling him what I thought of him, and as I was feeling by no means well, I think the sting of some of my pithy remarks will remain home for some time to come. I ended up by telling him that no Sergeant who had such ideas and dared to communicate them to other people deserved to hold their rank. He seemed quite penitent at last when I told him that if everyone went into battle with such ideas & wishes we should not uphold our name for fighting & lastly it was not our place to seek for peace at so early a stage of the war, but the Government's & if that body wanted us to go in, then we must not dispute it. But enough of this. I seem to be talking awful trash.

~

JANUARY 26 (TUESDAY) What has happened! Nine days and no entry in this journal. Well the fact of the matter is I have been too lazy. Have been orderly officer 8 times as the number of officers has been sadly decreased. I had to look after the Northumberland regiment for three days as no officer [of theirs] was present here. The weather was very wet & then the last few days has turned very cold. This morning awful frost. My sponge was frozen and refused to fulfill its duties. My shoes were so frozen that the laces would not do up, and my valise actually had a frost on the outside. My hair was very damp & I felt absolutely frozen.

My servant arrived at 8 A.M. & lit my charcoal in the frying pan. Soon the charcoal gave forth great heat & things started to melt a bit. I found out this first by some drops of water falling off the canvas on to my head & valise and as I did not want to get wet I had perforce to rise. My goodness, it was cold outside. But the washing was most exhilarating. I was on fatigue all day & we all worked a bit as it was too cold to stand about. At last I retired to bed early about 7 P.M. I shall never forget that evening. At 8 P.M. my lights were out & the moon shining brightly in the crisp atmosphere. The canteen (where the beer is sold) was just opened and the troops went in. The noise was indescribable. All drafts had gone out on the previous day and only the "details" were left, about 500 men, a few men in each regiment (those who have come back from hospital & are waiting their turn to go up to the front again). When they had all gone in, there was quiet for a few minutes while they drank (they had been paid out that afternoon). At last the beverage began to have its wont effect when drunk in quantities. First spontaneous noises arose, these died down in the pursuance of drinking. Suddenly raucous and forbidding singing arose. For my life, I could not help laughing, the noise was so indescribably funny. Picture to yourself many casks of beer in a huge marquee, several hundreds of men around drinking. Suddenly one gets up & sings, then all join in chorus & a hopeless melee of a dozen songs & jumbled into one suddenly is emitted.

As I lay in my valise I heard one man start singing "D'ye Ken John Peel, with his coat so gay," etc. After the first few verses of awful singing, quite out of tune, the chorus joined in with "Onward Christian Soldiers." The chorus had it all its way for a couple of minutes, when an individual with an awful stentorian voice yelled out "It's a long, long way to Tipperary." I think he was half drunk by his voice. Anyway he had a short life, because I heard an awful row & shouting & heard him no more. Doubtless some one angry at the ecclesiastical singing being interrupted threw a bottle at the singer & stopped him. The noise stopped and the crowd started singing quite a dozen different songs which made an awful noise. This was stopped by some one demanding for more beer & several others playing the mouth organ & Rattles. The sound seemed to employ the tune of "Oh! You beautiful doll." However I am not sure, as the ecclesiastical element started on "From Greenland's Icy Mountains," while half not liking the tune drifted on to "There is a green hill far away." This was again interrupted by a good many people yelling out oaths & shouting after the manner of people who are under the influence of too much beer. These people successfully stopped the singing & for about 2 minutes, shouting was the only thing. Then the singing started again & lasted about 15 minutes. Half hymns & half comic or well known songs. Then the end came. The chorus was singing "Jerusalem the Golden" when some ruffian yelled out (as far as I can remember) "You're no bally use, Joe, go and boil your _____ pate." Oaths followed much shouting & I believe the exit of several individuals. However, the fight [was] on, & I heard the "Guard" turn out & a general arrest started. This ended a most entertaining evening, as listening to this indescribable babble made one roar with laughter although one was in a tent. I thereupon rose & lit my candles & placing the whole thing on record as although it is impossible to set it down in writing & make it appear half as funny as it was, I was determined to write it down before I forget it.

～

JANUARY 27 (WEDNESDAY) Very odd. Heaps of Etonians arriving. Digby of the Coldstream Guards (Booker's house, Eton) left yesterday with 50 others & 100 men of the Guards, many drafts came in to-day, about 1500 I believe. Amongst the 60th Rifles I met Fowler awfully nice fellow whom I knew at Eton.* He was at Well's. There were also Sherlock of Somerville's & Hordein of Churchill's also at Eton. Hordein I knew very well, we went through the school together, & I like him immensely. Last of all! But wait a minute. A draft of the Black Watch 56 men with McFarlane, Murdock, & Haldane as officers arrived.† Haldane‡ is a nephew of the Chancellor Lord Haldane§ & was captain of the school at Eton being in college. He is immensely clever and was at Eton when I was there. He has already got his B.A. at Oxford. I sat next him at dinner & we enjoyed ourselves immensely going over reminiscences at Eton. He was a wet bob as I was. Haldane is not at all a stand-offish sort of person, but gives an appearance at first of being rather a fool. This is due to the fact that he laughs in an odd way & speaks oddly but really he is one of the nicest fellows going & his learning is very great. Luckily he does not air his knowledge, which is the hallmark of the true clever man. Many drafts have gone off this morning including 1st Black Watch under the command of McFarlane an awfully good

---

* Lt. G. G. Fowler died of wounds sustained at Loos, 26 September 1915.

† 2/Lt. R. McFarlane, 2/Lt. J. Murdoch.

‡ Lt. (later Captain) J. B. S. Haldane, twice wounded, survived the war to pursue a distinguished career as scientist, author, and professor of biochemistry and biology at Oxford and the University of London.

§ Viscount Richard Burton Haldane, lord chancellor from 1912 to 1915 and again in 1924, best known as the author of a series of far-reaching military reforms when Secretary for War (1905–1912).

fellow. Poor old Haldane has gone to hospital with a bad attack of influenza &
bronchitis. At 11 A.M. I was sent for by the Adjutant who informs me I am to
leave for the front to-night at 8 P.M. with 2/Lt. Ramsay as my second in
command. He is to go with the advance party of 4 men and 1 N.C.O. [non-
commissioned officer] to draw rations for us. He looks ill poor fellow. Has
Influenza so may go to hospital. I am writing this at 1 P.M., so the future is at
present unknown.

It's snowing hard now so it might be awfully cold in the train tonight. We shall
be in it in 24 hours they say. We entrain at the Gare Maritime. It's odd those this
morning entrained at Montvillier Station on a different line & right in the
country. This draft is going by itself accompanied by no others so I suppose it
will be a passenger train or a luggage train! with cattle trucks. I believe we are
going via Rouen, Boulogne, & Abbeville, & then at the end have a 12 mile romp
through the snow. I write below the last orders I receive at this depot at the Base.

> To be retained & shown on journey:
> Orders for officers 1/c of Reinforcements
> 1. Detail. The following details, strength 2 officers and 50 men other ranks,
> forming a reinforcement for 2d Black Watch will be held in readiness to
> proceed to the front to join .... Brigade 1st Division 1st Corps.
> 2. Guard. You will be held responsible for the above party & will place a guard
> on each van or compartment occupied by the men under your command to
> see that they do not straggle away and to maintain discipline generally. The
> strength of this guard to be at least 25% of the number of men in each van or
> compartment.
> 3. Report. On arrival at entraining point "Gare Maritime" you will report the
> arrival of your party to the D.A.D.R.T. [Deputy Assistant Director, Railway
> Transport] at 10 P.M.
> 4. "Haltes Repas." [meal stops] You will ascertain from the R.T.O. [Railway
> Transport Officer] before entraining the places of "Halte Repas," and the
> times of arrival and departure therefrom and will inform the details under
> your command.
> 5. Ration Statements. You will on arrival at Station be issued with 2 days'
> Rations and one day's Rations. You will therefore be rationed to 3 days from
> date of entrainment.

I am now drawing near to a close my sojourn at the base. What awaits me from
the time I leave the base, I do not know, and so it being a definite step forward
& of a different nature, its substance will be written in another book. However

there is still some space left. At 12 P.M. I went into the village & got some biscuits for the journey, and also looked into my photographers' shop to enquire after my photos.* Some have come out extraordinarily well, whereas others are useless, there being smudges on them, the whole film being covered with blotches of a green colour. Evidently I am not a very good photographer yet. However I think one photograph is excellent. Just finished lunch now and am going to pack my kit which has to be at the station by 4 P.M. I don't relish sorting out at all.

7.30 P.M. Am now ready for starting, having just dined. Packing was an effort. My valise is twice as large as when I brought it out. Weighs over 300 lbs, which is something over the prescribed weight by 200 lbs. I believe. My servant could hardly carry it. Ugh! it is cold. Snow everywhere but a moonlight night. Can one take a photo by moonlight, I wonder. Shall take 10 and await issue when I return to England if I ever do.

This little book, so precious to me I entrust to a Tommie's Haversack, part of my Webb† equipment I am not taking. Several other articles are also in the haversack. Thus may the Censor be taken in for once [and] allow its egress from France unsuspectingly. It is time to go as my watch says 7.45 P.M. so I must close this book and hope to write as legibly in the next as I have done here under the existing conditions.

I must now say good-by to the mess having been here just 4 weeks.

---

* Unfortunately, none of Lionel's photos have survived.
† Shoulder strapping with pouches for equipment.

3   Painful Journey

27 January–1 February 1915

JANUARY 27 Evening. What an odd thing. Now I have landed in this odd station, I have clean forgotten if to-day is Tuesday or Wednesday, nobody can enlighten me so I will assume it's Tuesday.* What a lot has happened since I wrote last in my little journal. Here I am seat[ed] on my valise in a draughty & cold shed called the Gare Maritime. There is much snow about & things look rotten, but I was never in better spirits. It's most odd and what has happened in the last few hours would be enough to dishearten anyone. It is now 1.30 A.M. and cold. I believe that I forgot to say in the other journal that a clergyman, finding me in the mess at 6 P.M., I think, with several others, on finding out that I was off to the front, declared his intention of giving a service. So a service was given. An awful hailstorm prevailed and made such a noise on the tin roof that the preacher could only say a few words a minute. Never shall I forget that service, held in the flickering firelight, a snow & hailstorm without, and I off to the front in 2 hours' time. He finished and gave me a small prayer which he said Lord Roberts had given him. It was printed and I still retain it. I shall value it. I went out at 7.45 P.M. to put on my equipment and got soaked in an awful rain and hailstorm. I at length found my tent & with my servant's aid succeeded in putting on my kit. My revolver refused to fit on to the "Webb" & slung itself upside down. At length my kit being assembled I essayed to emerge from my tent. Now overlooked the fact that having a very heavy pack on my back I was top-heavy. So having got caught up in the tent mouth, I emerged with violence, tripped up on the inner flap and fell face in the mud my left hand being undermost. My finger or thumb doubled under, and an awful pain resulted. I managed to get down to the parade ground 1 minute late, & waited for the Adjutant to come. He came & said we could leave. We marched off in total darkness. My thumb-finger hurt me abominably, and trying to take off my glove, found it impossible as it had swollen

---

* It was Wednesday.

so. We marched to the Gare Maritime about 5 miles & arrived there about 9 P.M. There I found Wilson of the Camerons who had conducted my advance party down to draw rations as Ramsay was ill & could not come. On the way down my shoes hurt me considerably & I determined to go to the Ordnance Stores & draw another pair of boots. My first pair were unlucky as I lost them. I left my sergeant (McWilliams) in charge of the 50 men and gave him my paper in case he was asked for it by anyone. I then got into a taxi that had by chance brought some other officers & we told the chap to drive to the Ordnance Retail Stores, intending afterwards to have my hand seen to, as it was very inflamed. We reached the Ordnance after sometime & told the taxi to wait 5 minutes for us. We went in and got a large pair of boots and a second pair of socks, so as to have plenty of room. Two other fellows came in and asked for some revolver cartridges. They soon went out however. After 10 minutes we went outside to proceed into the town in our taxi. What was our dismay to find the taxi gone. Evidently those other freaks had taken it. It seems a very unlucky evening. We went into the Ordnance again and asked them to ring up a taxi for us. They took 10 minutes to do it, so we got angry & left. We had to trek back to the Gare Maritime, which was a good 3 miles away [and got] lost somewhere in the docks, amid the confusing lights. It was 10 P.M. by now, the time when I should have reported to the R.T.O. concerning my draft, but my hand hurt awfully, so I decided I must have that seen to first. By 11.15 P.M. after much wandering getting lost we found the awful "Gare." I spotted a coffee stall & a Red Cross Nurse, so I made a beeline for her & she offered to attend to the thumb. I explained that I did not mind it hurting provided I could only get my glove on. She said she thought I had splintered the bone or something & said I ought to have it X-rayed, but such a tragedy I did not want to have happen, so I let the matter slide.* She however bound up the thumb having heated it & then poured cold water over it. After that I set out to find the R.T.O. to report. At 12 P.M. I found him and he informed me I was late. I explained that I had arrived at 9 P.M. but had had my hand seen to. He then said the train went at 12.49 midnight. My next step was to find my men. These I discovered in two cattle trucks laying down amongst the hay. They seemed very philosophical. I then sat down on my baggage in the draughts & wrote this. Hullo! 1 A.M. and not off yet! At 12.49 punctually they sent our two coaches up and down shunting us about with no apparent reason other than to annoy us. My candle which I had established on the window sill fell off heralding the charge of the engine against the carriage. It was curious to notice, but not to

---

* Lionel probably considers the "tragedy" to be any procedure that would delay his trek to the front.

endure, that whenever we were shunted about the engine sort of ran at us & charged us about. This shunting is still going on as I write & I fill in on moments when it stops shunting. I have a fairly comfortable compartment with 2 others who are going to the front.

Hullo! 2.15 A.M. just off so can't write more.

~

JANUARY 28 (THURSDAY) It is now 8 A.M. in the morning, what a night to be sure. We never exceeded 15 miles an hour the whole of our journey to this place, Rouen. We stopped quite 40 times and once right in the middle of a tunnel for half an hour. I don't think anyone slept at all. The first intimation we had of being in Rouen was just after we had halted on a bridge presumably [over] the Seine and when we advanced again we swayed so much that we thought we were off the lines. We progressed a little further & got shunted about among a goods yard, and at last the engine having played with us enough, ran off & deserted. Some ass came and yelled in at the window. We told him to shut up and I asked him if the Black Watch were still on board as I had misgivings that their trucks had been lost during the previous night's orgy of shunting. The fellow looked half daft & said something about it being his watch now & would hear in the morning. I got bored with him and shoved him off the sideboards. An official then came and said we should remain there till 10 A.M. in the morning when we were to report to the R.T.O. for further instructions. It was then 5.15 A.M. So there was nothing to do but to try and sleep till daybreak. At 8 A.M. I awoke & was keen to take a photograph, so I asked my 2 companions what exposures to give, they did not know, so I took two snapshots, one a 8 second exposure and the other 12 seconds. I haven't the faintest idea what the result will be, as the sky was so odd. I am just going to read up my little photography book. It's a most odd thing in what good spirits I am. I seem to be looking forward to something I know not what.

9.15 A.M. Have just taken a little walk in and out of the trucks & have spoken to my men who are also in good spirits. I met a fellow of the 93rd (2nd Battalion of Arg & Suth Hds) who is here on fatigue work. He told me that there is a large draft of our men in Rouen and about 4 officers, all from the 4th Battalion, so I suppose the two Tysons, Duff and Merrilees, are among them.* My thumb hurts awfully today. Luckily it's not my right hand or I should be unable to write.

---

* J. D. Tyson, A. B. Tyson, T. R. Duff, and S. B. Merrilees.

These last few pages must sound very odd as I jot down items every few hours, thus I shall have a very complete record of my journey to the trenches.

12 P.M. What a monotonous day. It has only had one relieving feature so far.

At 10 A.M. I went out & found a sort of refreshment room, where I procured some biscuits and hot tea. Many of the Argylls were there and I noticed that although they were on fatigue work they were all congregated together amongst the refreshments. I had a long talk with them and was especially pleased to meet Pvt. Murray of my old Platoon & also Pvt. Lamont of A Co'y which is also the Company I was in. We had some interesting talks together, and they informed me that Captain Chrystol of the 4th Argylls had already gone out, indeed with the last draft of 100 men. He had so it appeared already gone up to the firing line. I then proceeded, on being asked by a very nice young lady to enter a back portion of the building where one could drink one's tea away from the men. From her I learnt that this refreshment place at Rouen was an entirely private concern run by Lady someone or other, who also helped to serve, indeed there were quite 5 ladies helping, and they were all English. The whole place was made up of curious wooden compartments. Having enjoyed myself immensely I went out to see the R.T.O. about the continuance of my journey. Outside his office there were 3 Indians, all looking more or less dilapidated. I went in and the officer told me I should proceed at 7 P.M. on the remainder of my journey. The detachment of 50 men & 1 officer to be in truck 33. I suppose I shall have a 1st class compartment again later on. The matter being disposed of satisfactorily, another fellow joined me and we took a walk on the line. I took some more photographs and my friend told me I should only give an exposure of 2 seconds. So I suppose my other photographs, the exposures being 8 & 12 respectively will not appear, anyway it will be interesting to see later. I took the last photo from an empty carriage, shutting the door so as to keep the camera steady; suddenly we felt a bump, the camera jumped out of my hands & fell on to the ground outside, while our train was suddenly in motion, we having not noticed that an engine was just going to be attached. The door refused to open until the carriages were running too swiftly to allow of jumping without a certain amount of risk. So we sat tight, hoping not to be taken back to Le Havre again. After a brisk run of about 10 minutes or so the train stopped, we jumped out & tried to explain to the engine driver, but we found no engine, the train must have been shunted from some way back, so the only thing left to do was to trek it back. We were held up 4 times by the French sentries who wanted to arrest us, but I produced my entraining orders and although they couldn't understand them, they quietened the sentries down at once. We soon arrived at the spot of our sudden involuntary departure. The camera was there, a little dented, but serviceable I think, for I pressed the trigger and it worked, but I then found out I had wasted another photograph as the instrument was pointing to the ground. We then returned, each to our carriage & rested.

It is now 7 P.M. and I have seen all my men into the train which I believe starts 8 P.M., whether it travels via Amiens, or Dieppe I do not know, but I am sure we visit Boulogne. I stayed in my train all afternoon and evening and suffered the inconvenience of being shunted about in order to form a new train. I must have gone up and down quite 20 times but I could not go & see the town because of having my men here. I took many photographs during the day of various views as seen when I was shunted about. I however just missed photographing a huge train of Belgian refugees from La Bassée. Also a trainload of wounded Indians.

What is today by the way, I believe it's Wednesday the 28th.* Therefore tomorrow is the 29th.

Hullo! Thursday† is upon us, it's now 9.30 A.M. and I believe we have to report to the R.T.O. at 10.30 A.M. for further orders. We are shunted into a huge goods yard again, as at Rouen, & absolutely surrounded by vans. A Red Cross hospital train is on our right. How wounded get on board I do not know as it is the permanent way. It's raining hard now. I suppose I shall eat biscuits today as yesterday. It took us 12 hours to get from Rouen here about 130 miles. A bit slow it seems to me. We travelled via Amiens, Abbeville and Etaples, starting at 7.30 P.M. and arriving 8 A.M. today.

Have suddenly remembered my Father is in Boulogne with his car on ambulance work, perhaps I shall be able to look him up.

Well it is now 11 P.M. and a very enjoyable day I've had too.

The train was shunted through the town choosing a very crowded street to do so, and was then halted miles away in another goods' yard a few yards from the sea. We then went to the R.T.O.'s office & reported. I wrote my name down in a book & he said Report yourself or telephone "20 Military" at 2.30 P.M. & you will be told what time you are to leave. Well as I am very tired I intend giving a very short survey of the day's doings. I knew Father was in the British Red Cross

---

* Lionel is still confused. It was Thursday 28 January.
† No, it was Friday!

Society so I set out to find it. I found it eventually. They had taken possession of the Hôtel de Paris & intend entering the Hôtel Chrystol later on. He was not there, so leaving word I walked the streets in the hopes of meeting him. I entered a chemist and had my hand re-bandaged up, as it was most painful. I walked all over the town and saw the castle and cathedral. Everybody thought I was wounded from the front from the appearance of my bandaged hand. At 12 noon I returned & found father in his room. Very dark, but quite nice after tents. He then took me to see some colonel (a Doctor) about my hand as it was much painful. He told me to use it as little as possible & re-bandaged it again, with some cotton wool as well. We then had lunch together down below, and I was introduced to various people of the Red X [Cross] Society. After lunch I enquired about my train & I paid a visit to an army dentist in one of the hospitals, a place which had formerly been a truck shed. Father had his seen to and then mine. We were examined, nothing was wrong however. Very good teeth, he said. We then departed and Father suggested a drive. So we drove in the ambulance car to Wimereux and beyond passing three barriers with sentries. We saw many hospitals on the way. We returned a different way covering in all about 12 miles. We then had tea and afterwards took a walk to buy some things. Father then bought 18 francs' worth of chocolate for my men. Very kind of him. We returned, had din[n]er & then I met a very good fellow, name I forget, Holt or something like that, a member of the family or a great friend. I liked him. After dinner we packed up the various things bought in the stores, & at 8.45 P.M. set out for the train. After much hunting about in a drenching rain, by the way it had poured all day with an awful wind, we found my coach & the vans with the men. The chocolate was doled out & we sought my carriage. I lit my "reschau du soldat" & heated my coat, which soon got dried. At 10 P.M. the train showed signs of moving so saying "good-by" to Father & my friend, they went away and at 11 P.M. [I] started to write. The train stopped me at intervals as it would start & halt. I have just finished this writing now at 11.45 P.M. while the train is apparently "dormant" in a street.

By the way my sergeant McWilliams has just brought me a crime* made out against 3 of my men, who put into the town this afternoon & were accused of pocketing a bottle of wine. I am sorry for the men as to be confined in a train for 48 hours is no joke, and I am prepared to be lenient, as we are at the end of the journey. If we were going to have another long stop like this, I should make an example of them, to stop it occurring again, but as we shall be at the front in the morning, & as I know what it is for a man to start badly with a

---

* A crime sheet, a notice of some infraction of military regulation.

Map 2. The northern section of the Western Front in 1915.

crime against him, I will let them off. I told McWilliams that & he was pleased. I shall give them a good lecture in the morning however. I am taking full responsibility for tearing up the crime, but I am prepared & do not mind what anybody may say as I think I have done right. We are off now as my writing must show, so I must stop.

∽

JANUARY 30 (SATURDAY) 8.30 A.M. now. We arrived here at Chocques (gives one a choking feeling to say it) at 6.30 A.M. and can go no farther because some Germans here have blown up the line by Béthune they tell us. Chocques is a small village situated 3 miles west of Béthune and at present about 4½ miles from the firing line by La Bassée.* We can hear no firing at present, perhaps they are having their breakfast. We arrived at this spot after passing through the towns and villages of Lamer, Despones, Lumbres, St. Omer, & Aire, and here we are! It was a beautiful moonlight night & today has the appearance of being very fine & likely to be useful for photographs. At 7.30 I went outside and was told by an R.T.O. that we must walk to Béthune later on perhaps 9 A.M. I then searched about for a washing place and after passing through the station found a pump on the platform. I divested myself & had a good wash. By now some of [the] men had come up and they also indulged in ablutions, so I took several photographs including one of my sergeant McWilliams. Returning I lit my "reschau du soldat" & boiled some chocolate and a fine drink it made too. My servant Vallance & McWilliams indulged in this beverage as well. Hullo! the R.T.O. has come and told us to shift so I must stop 8.45 A.M.

Having left Chocques we marched to Béthune, passing quantities of cars, etc. on way. The road was cobbled & was very bad to walk on. I reported myself at Béthune & my men were then allotted to their different companies. I then went past Beuvry close to the German lines & was there till January 31st, being part of the time in Beuvry. Little happened, there was plenty of rifle fire and shells galore, but you get used to them. Beuvry was heavily shelled on the 31st, & on the 1st of February we returned to Béthune, which is only 4 or 5 miles from the firing line.

---

* See map of Béthune (support area), p. 35.

4 Just Behind the Front Lines

2–6 February 1915

FEBRUARY 2 (TUESDAY) At last a little time to write. The bustle of the last few days and the impossibility of writing has naturally rendered my diary short. To-day I learn that owing to the heavy casualties in the first division we are to rest for 3 weeks or so, & then go up again. We have sent our billeting officers up today. In the recent fighting we have lost 7 officers and about 300 men.* We now have only 12 officers in the battalion.

It's odd isn't it. I am now in the 1st Battalion of the Black Watch. I have again been posted to a different regiment. Was first in the Argyll's, was then for a month in the 2nd Black Watch at Le Havre, and am now in the 1st Battalion. My address should now be if made public:

> 2/Lt. L. F. Sotheby
> 1st Black Watch
> 1st Division
> 1st Corps
> 1st Brigade.

Sounds well, doesn't it. First in everything. All the best regiments are in the 1st Division (all the Guard's) etc.† I believe we are going to Lillers or some place to re-fit and organize the men again. Lillers is N.W. of Béthune and is about 13 miles from the firing line. I walked towards Beuvry this morning and then on towards La Bassée. I reached our guns and talked to many of the men about.

---

* The unit history lists the casualties as 6 officers and 205 other ranks. A. G. Wauchope, *A History of the Black Watch [Royal Highlanders] in the Great War, 1914–1918*, 3 vols. (London, 1926), 1:32.

† The First Division included the 1st (Guards) Brigade, comprised of the 1/Coldstream Guards, 1/Scots Guards, 1/Camerons, Lionel's 1/Black Watch, and a Territorial unit, 1/14th London Scottish.

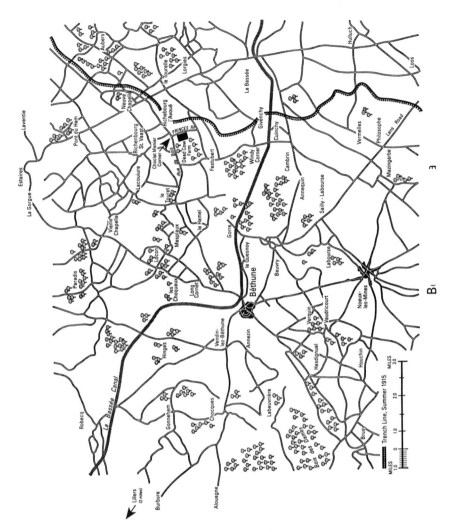

Map 3. Béthune (support) area.

Very little was doing and only a few shells were flying about. Many officers had walked out from Béthune to see if any progress had been made. Everyone was joking and it seemed too ridiculous that that cobbled road from Béthune led right into the trenches a few yards away and then on into the Germans.

It was about 12 noon. Then I suddenly met Nash[*] and Johnstone on bykes.

---

[*] Capt. L. C. Nash, K.R.R.C., died of wounds sustained at Loos, 28 September 1915.

They are old Etonians and I saw them down at the base only a few days ago. They had been in all that fierce fighting too, & had come up now, the same as I, to see if anything was doing. The German trenches were out of sight, the other side of a dip in the ground. I returned soon, and then whom should I meet in the town of Beuvry but Fowler, another Etonian in the 60th Rifles. He was quite well. Later on I met Sudbury of the Royal Sussex, who had also been at the base with me. I was very sorry to hear from him that in that fierce fighting Granshaw had been killed, shot in the stomach and Barthrop had died of wounds in the head while firing. I knew both very well at the base at Le Havre, and was immensely sorry to hear of their death. I got to know a tremendous amount of officers at that Base, quite 200 I should think, and day by day, I see their deaths or wounds recorded in the paper. It's awful in a way and yet I am revelling in it, and would not have peace declared for any money. It's simply heavenly this life. I suppose my exuberance will wear off in time, but at present nothing can stay it.

I have now been on active service for about 5 weeks in France and in England on home defence work on the south and then the N East coast for 5 months approximately. Thus I have had no leave for about 6½ months. Most fellows have had leave twice in that time. But I do not think I will apply for any leave yet.

Béthune was shelled the other day when we were close by. Many people were wounded and a shell bursting on a large stable killed many horses.

It's extraordinary, here one is 4 miles from the firing line, and yet everyone is living as if nothing had happened, or was about to happen. In the afternoon I went into the town with another fellow, and entered a Café close by the square. I had luncheon there, my first day on arriving here and then enjoyed it. The couple who keep the Café or restaurant have a very pretty daughter there who waits on you, and she is all the more pleasant because she is not like most other French girls I have seen so far, who smile and try to talk at once and familiarly with you if you are in a kilt (especially). She is most demure and quiet and not habituated like the fast French girls, indeed this one in her simplicity and neatness is far, far more attractive and would make a most excellent companion to talk to, as one could almost imagine she was English, and with the better views of an English girl. So after we left, my companion went off, and I returned to have a cup of chocolate, & try to talk some French if possible. I spent a most agreeable 2 hours there, and the more I saw her, the more I liked her for her extreme decency in every way. It was a great relief to be able to speak to some one feminine who was of a nice sort and not of the usual French town type. I got on famously with my French &

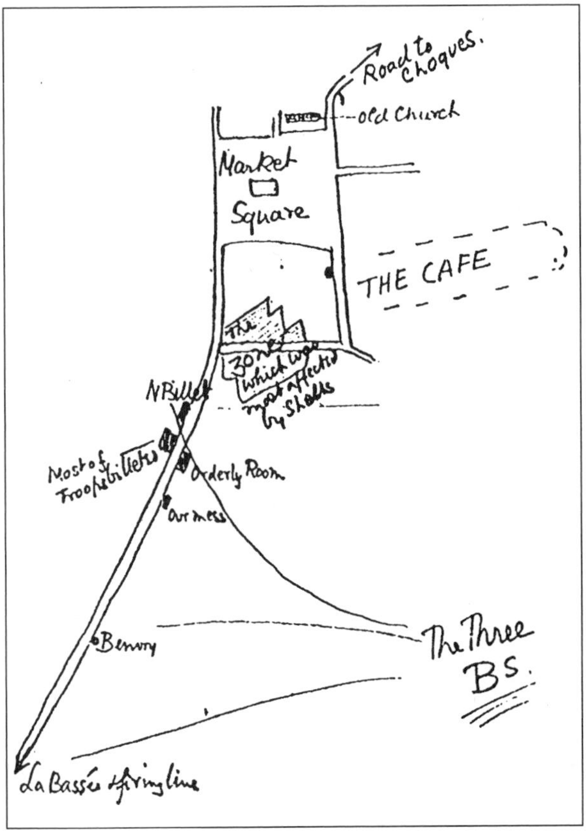

Road to choques.

old Church

Market Square

THE CAFE

zone in which were most affected by shells

N Bull

Most of Troops billets

Orderly Room

our mess

Bemmy

La Bassé springline

The Three B S.

Map 4. Lionel's hand-drawn plan of Béthune and Linette's café.

half English and she in her turn, and indeed I shall never forget that splendid time we had together for a short time, as I suppose I shall see much rough life before I get home. I am not ashamed to put this little episode in because as I am writing a diary of all facts that happen and perfectly sound not leaving hardly anything out; unless I forget or have no time, I put in everything. I especially lay stress on my short meeting in the Café because I enjoyed myself immensely, as the girl in question was of the type I most like, quiet but lively when necessary, graceful, with no silly speech, courteous, and extremely well mannered, indeed from her refinement I should have thought she was a thorough lady. I am indeed sorry to leave tomorrow, if we have to and I told her so, whereat she made some very pleasing phrases. I shall never forget that Café & her 2 hours' society among the raging world so desperate all round. Her name was Linette, and very nice too. Here is a plan of where the Café is, should anyone ever visit Béthune after the war is over.

The map of the town of Béthune is meant to show various parts of interest including the part most affected by the recent shelling.

I should just like to mention the fact that I visited the very old church. It is most beautiful and must be most aged, perhaps the 13th century. Its tower is massive and very thick standing close on 200 feet off the ground I should judge. I wonder that the Germans have not shelled it. It is a great landmark on this flat country and a great observation post. I think it proves that the Germans do not make a habit of bombarding churches, and that perhaps the papers exaggerate too much when they talk of the Germans' so-called "atrocities." After all it is very easy for a shell to strike a church by mistake and to cause so much damage as to lead one to expect many shells had fallen.

I returned to my billet after looking at an enormous hole caused by a Jack Johnson or Black Maria. It's just about 7.30 P.M. now, so I must leave off & go to mess.

❧

FEBRUARY 4 (THURSDAY) 2.30 P.M. We have now been in this little village of Burbure 1 hour. We left Béthune at 9.30 A.M. There was a terrific cannonade going on at La Bassée & our guns were making a tremendous noise. Our guns I suppose are only 1½ miles distant from Béthune in one place. The regiment was formed up in the street and I was told to join D Company for the march out. 2/Lt. McKenzie is in command of it.[*] I knew him at the Base some time ago. By the way I have forgotten to mention that I have found in the Battalion several fellows who I know. Major Hamilton, 2/Lts. McFarlane and McKenzie & Lt. Richard also a Captain Green.[†] All these were at the Base with me earlier in the year. Captain Skene who I also knew at the Base is now wounded.[‡]

Well we marched off, D Company leading, I in charge of No. 14 Platoon. We had 5 Pipers in front with one soldier who carried our standard with the 42nd on it. The Pipe Major was wounded the other day, and several other pipers killed. One set of pipes lost in the action was found & returned to the regiment yesterday. Well we marched off & went right through the town coming

---

[*] 2/Lt. R. I. McKenzie, who had just arrived 10 January, died of wounds two months later, 10 April 1915.

[†] Major J. G. H. Hamilton, second in command of the battalion; 2/Lt. R. MacFarlane, later transferred to 2nd Battalion and promoted to captain, was killed in April 1916 at the Battle of Istabulat in Mesopotamia; 2/Lt. J. E. M. Richard; Capt. W. Green.

[‡] Captain P. G. M. Skene was wounded the afternoon of 25 January in the battle for Givenchy.

out at the far end opposite to Chocques. We attracted much attention as several fellows were tied up with bandages & I had my hand all bandaged as the old place had reopened & the thumb at the joint looks bored with life & behaves badly. We passed convoy after convoy of troops and cars & ammunitions and supplies. Indians, the Gurkhas & Sikhs, were driving most of the carts, some having very small carts, drawn by two small ponies. On entering Chocques we passed a long train of ours. Guns of all sorts and looking very fit and able to do their good work. They took up nearly half a mile of the road. I took many photos en route. Passing under the railway bridge an armoured train rushed by. Three guns with enormous long muzzles projecting were seated on platforms and able to swing round in any position; a very small and insignificant engine drew them, but they sped at quite 40 miles an hour in the direction of Béthune, going perhaps to give the Germans a quick attack by Givenchy (1 km west of La Bassée) and then rush back. They do this every day and a gun was wrecked the other day. We were a very long line stretching nearly ¾ of a mile, though we were only about 750 strong, but then of course we had 4 kitchens (on wheels), our watercarts, our transport carts and the like, following in our wake. I took several photos, which if they come out, will be a pleasant reminiscence to keep. After passing along a very straight road with magnificent trees we left the hard cobbled stones which cut one's feet so, and came onto a softer road, thus saving our feet, but making us in a dirty state. This lasted till the village of Allouagne was reached, here it may be interesting to note we were billeted [with] the North Lancashire regiment (information of this kind would never pass the Censor). Passing through this village, we struck N.W. and went over one of the most awful roads I have ever seen. It is marked on the map as not being much of a road, but today, well! it was atrocious. One slid into mud-holes at the slightest invitation to firm ground. The C.O. called a halt half way across this morass to give us a rest. So we all stuck there and wallowed about, shifting from one position to another in order not to sink too far. The baggage carts looked awfully fed up. We at length ploughed on through still more liquid mud and eventually reached the village of Burbure on a small rise of ground. We passed through till we reached the large square in the centre & there each company filed off to different positions to be billeted. Each water cart and each kitchen following their respective companies.

The following letter, misdated 7 January, most certainly refers to events just described in the diary as taking place on 4 February. The letter, though addressed to no one in particular, was most likely to Lionel's mother, and probably written from Burbure on 7 February 1915. The deletions here are probably by Lionel, on this occasion censoring his own account. Later letters, however, do not always display such circumspection.

We were waiting orders at _____ to march into billets at _____ and on the _____ at _____ in the morning we marched off. The sun was shining brilliantly and everywhere was peace and calm, except for the crash and boom of guns 2 miles away. We marched through the straggling town the inhabitants flocking to see the "Kilties!" Four pipers were in front, the others being killed or wounded. They made a good sight. A battalion many hundreds strong were we, few officers in truth, & depleted in ranks but as strong as strong could be. Out of the village we filed, D, B, C, A platoons and sections intermingled, along the cobbled road leading to _____. We passed Indians and transports galore, and then marching through _____ and on for some time, we passed into mud and slime, and by 2.30 P.M. arrived at _____. There was a beautiful common there, oblong in shape and at both ends of one diagonal there were pools.

On to the common we filed, each company going to its allotted portion. Each field kitchen following its company, and the transport and water carts drawing up the centre. We billet. The men are warned that if they get drunk, worse quarters will be found them. Hay lofts are used and all outbuildings. The houses are mostly one floors, with hay lofts above. The outhouses queer barns with mud walls and floors feet deep in straw. The upper storeys appeared to be in senile decay, 5 or 6 long branches thrown across some beams and straw atop; that is the ceiling for one room and the floor for another.

The first accident soon came, as ladders have to be used to ascend. There was only one ladder for 5 lofts, so struggles ensued. One lot captured the ladder, and one man ascended. The top rung broke and down he came, everyone hugely delighted, one loft was so bad that the men used to keep falling through the ceiling, as fast as they reached their upper room. However they are happy, and it is only their obstinate coughs which cause one pain, as it is awful to hear them.

My word, this village is old. There was awful trouble this morning because the alarm was raised in one billet and the guard turned out. Apparently one of the fellows had gone to draw water and the boards gave way, precipitating him into the well, about 15 feet down. He yelled and shouted and men came up. He was incoherent and swinging about. Someone said Germans, and the alarm was raised. At last a sergeant let down a rope with a bucket and the figure came up sitting in the bucket. Order was quickly resumed. Hundreds of things like this happened.

Good, I have discovered a man who develops photographs, a miner. He spends 2 P.M. till 2 A.M. in the coal mine, and is up the rest. My photographs are developing well.

We have about two weeks rest I think, but vary on drill all the time. Beautiful country for it. We hear the guns all day, being only 12 miles from the firing line. Aeroplanes constantly hover around, and white puffs denote where shells burst close up to them. These puffs remain hours at a time quite stationery. Canons are mounted on turrets and small lines, these recede into the side of a hill and can rush out and fire, and then rush in again. Very safe, they command all valleys.

Well, it is time for a parade now.

[unsigned]

FEBRUARY 4 (THURSDAY) [Diary resumes] I was at present, and had been for the last week or so, served with D Company. A word here is necessary. D Company lost its company commander and two of its platoon commanders in the awful fighting recently round La Bassée and consequently 2/Lt. Mackenzie was placed in command temporarily.[*] Major Murray will be in command tomorrow I expect, as he is the junior major.[†] In the recent engagement Mackenzie and his batman were the sole survivors. Wonderful somehow he escaped without a wound though a bullet passed through his glengarry. The bullets & shells were whistling about and yet they escaped. Those two companies[‡] got it in the neck "ganz und gar" [thoroughly] as the Germans would say. Mackenzie is an awfully nice fellow and was at Sandhurst. He is in one of the photographs I took today. I only hope that he will escape, though there is little chance of any of us ever getting through in the face of the awful slaughter that is about to come soon now. When we advance we will be falling just as when a mowing machine is hacking at the corn, falling in sheaves practically speaking. Whole regiments will be blown to hell, just as the Germans have been when they attacked us. It will be just the same only we shall be the losers. The retreat of the

---

[*] Captain H. F. S. Amery had earlier commanded D Company, was wounded at the Aisne in September 1914, recovered, and returned to the company on 1 November to take command of C Company. He was again wounded the very next day during the fighting at Ypres—so severely that he was returned to England, where he was hospitalized and died several months later.

[†] Major James Thomas (Crockatt) Murray, a veteran of the Black Watch since 1893, took over command of the battalion after the death of Lt. Col. Adrian Grant-Duff, killed at the Aisne 14 September 1914. Murray commanded the battalion only six weeks when he was himself wounded 1 November and did not return to duty until 4 February 1915, when he had to settle for command of D Company instead of the battalion.

[‡] B and D Companies.

Germans will not be disorderly very probably, I think they will contest every acre of ground, and as they have good trenches, well sited & with good fields of fire, they will mow us down and with small losses to themselves, I think. By now they will have chosen their positions with the eyes of experts and will have guns trained on possible places of attack. To drive the Germans out of Belgium and of west France I think that from now, we shall at the lowest figure lose a million men. Yes, I know the figure is large to people outside, but to anyone who knows the Germans, their obstinacy, pluck, endurance and marvelous patriotism, men who for their country are content to be slaughtered like a hundred sparrows in line if a gun is fired at them from the side, it is the lowest figure one could place. I may be wrong, but I doubt. More will be needed I think. To reach the Rhine will be our utmost I think.

Well, to return, after seeing D Co'y all billeted, I found my billet and shook my things down. I then saw the C.O. and he told me I was now attached to A Company. I have now been in two companies of the Black Watch. I accordingly hurried round and found Captain Evans arranging their billets.* Richard (lieutenant) was also there. After that I was with Shand (2/Lt.) for about 2 hours. Shand is an awfully good sort and seen fighting for months now. I like him immensely. He has had many escapes. Recently a bullet seared his coat from top to bottom somehow.† I ate some chocolate for lunch. By the way we arrived here about 2 P.M. having travelled on foot since 9.30 A.M. At 4 P.M. took a walk with Murdoch (2/Lt.) who has also seen fighting before & was wounded.‡ I had left him behind at the base with Major Murray. He was here when we arrived. Major Murray will take command of D Company now I suppose.

We walked to the west of the town & nearly to the main road which goes from Lillers to St. Pol. Much traffic was passing and many ambulances. We returned at 5 P.M., & I took my photos to be developed close by. At 7 P.M. I retired, having eaten all 3 meals of chocolate. By the way at 3 P.M., orderly room, D Company was ordered up in fatigue dress and a prisoner brought up from the Guard Room between two men with fixed bayonets. It was the promulgation of sentence of a court martial. The men were formed up so: men on three sides, escort & accused in centre, adjutant on left; he read out the sentence, two years' imprisonment hard labour. I am told, however, he will probably get three

---

* Captain L. P. Evans, one of four Black Watch to receive the coveted Victoria Cross (at Passchendaele, 1917), was to take command of the 1st Battalion in January 1918 and in June, to command the 14th Infantry Brigade. He survived the war.

† 2/Lt. A. Shand, killed at Aubers Ridge, 9 May 1915.

‡ 2/Lt. J. Murdoch, wounded again at Aubers Ridge, 9 May 1915.

weeks and will then be sent to the front again. A fine fellow he was too. Probably a small offense, but then all offenses are magnified here. Well, am off to bed now as am very tired.

~

FEBRUARY 5 (FRIDAY) It is now 5 P.M. & I start to recount the day's work. I now find that I am in B Company where I am apparently to remain. Officially I have No. 5 Platoon, but am at present second in command of the Company. I woke up at 4 A.M. as indeed did most people, as there was a most terrific cannonade going on, the noise was quite deafening although a little distance away. They seemed to be firing to the left & right of Béthune, & then coming with a great sweep into France, practically behind us by St. Pol. Thus although we are only about 12 miles from the firing line N of Béthune, S.E. we are barely 7 miles. It was a beautiful morning and as bright as day with the moon shining. The flashes of the guns could be plainly seen & the shells as they burst. Mingled amongst all this hurly burly one could plainly distinguish the pop, pop, pop, of machine guns (rapid fire). They have a noise peculiar to themselves. After a bit as no shells were bursting by the village, I retired to rest. I am always wondering if they will run an armoured train down here and shell us one night. This is possible as German aeroplanes were out today scouting & we saw some almost overhead at about 11.30 A.M. They were however briskly fired at by our guns at Béthune & at other places, but they will have an idea of our whereabouts as we were all out doing various drills at the time. The Coldstream Guards are close by too, at the other end of the village in fact. They got smashed up the other day in the fighting on the 25th January, the "Bloody Day," as people here call it. They saw red & went "hell for leather" at the Germans, doing awful execution. They were, however, cut up once as the Germans caught them napping, while drawing rations.

At 7.45 A.M. I got up and went without breakfast as I was not hungry. Ate some chocolate for breakfast instead. I went to the billets of my men practically opposite and there met my commander Lieutenant Edwards.* "B" and "D" Companies were the ones that suffered most in the recent heavy fighting at Givenchy, 3 miles east of Béthune. Most of my draft of 50 and Sergeant McWilliams, who came with it, were also quartered in the billets & had been attached to that company (B). I reported myself and we went and lectured all our N.C.O.s in a barn. The lecture was from printed matter given in from the

---

* Lt. W. H. C. Edwards, killed at Aubers Ridge, 9 May 1915.

brigadier whose name is Lowther (Scot's Guards).[*] He had apparently got it a bit hot from headquarters as our brigade had not done as well as had been intended. Bad luck on him as he looks a nice sort of man & his brigade major looks similar. I met them later on. The gist of the lecture was that Headquarters considers the Division (I) in general was a bit demoralized. It's no good mincing matters and keeping it back, for this diary is as true as it is possible to be. The lecture said that too many requests were given the men and too few orders. Result, not much done. A good deal of ammunition had been wasted by carelessly throwing it away. In fact altogether not a very favourable report, but I think our men have done very well, as they certainly did at the last great fight at Givenchy and at the subsequent encounters of lesser importance. The men certainly look very fit and except for the awful coughs they have, rather dirty overcoats and balaclava helmets, one considers them the flower of the army. The lecture being given, and only interrupted once by a corporal who started swearing outside because he went up to his thigh nearly in horse slush and filth and then fell flat on his face splashing filth in every direction, we filed out and a parade was formed. We went through a small lecture on interior economy & discipline and drifted on to section training. The platoons were split up and section training was gone through till 10.30 A.M. Brigadier Lowther and his major then came and spoke to us, seemed quite pleased, & rode off. Later I heard he had cursed some fellows for bad drill. I am awfully sorry I did not have my camera then as the sun shining right on him would have made a beautiful photograph. He looked superb on his steed & cap with gold and scarlet.

I then sat on a small haystack with Edwards and looked towards La Bassée where heavy fighting was going on. One could see the huge puffs of white smoke break into being in the air, denoting where a shell had been fired at an aeroplane. Suddenly two German ones appeared quite close to our village of Burbure. Heavy firing told us of their approach. They were being chased. However they got near enough to take topographical & useful knowledge & then fled off towards St. Pol or Arras, where they crossed our lines again. We must have seen quite 15 puffs of white smoke break and envelop them. They then disappeared, winged or not I know not. These white clouds hung about for an hour and drifted overhead within 5 minutes as a South Easterly breeze was blowing. A wonderful day, clear except for a slight haze near the firing line and the coal pit chimneys to the left belching forth grimy black smoke. A spectacle truly wonderful and worthy of a painting by Titian or Kreuz my favourite painter, a

---

* Brig-Gen. H. C. Lowther.

Frenchman who painted a beautiful painting called "Das Junges Madelien," "The Young Girl," a picture which is (a copy perhaps) in the Kaiser Frederick Museum in Berlin.* I adore that picture & would love to bag it from Berlin if we enter that city. I remember visiting the Kaiser Frederick Museum scores of times simply and solely to see my favourite one. One indeed if I remember in times of stress I shall never forget. Well, rather wandering from the point, am I not, but Kreuz I should like to meet as his painting I adore.

Well, the sun was beaming down, and yet with all this intoxicating liveliness and loveliness of country, men were going and taking lives a few miles away. This life I am simply adoring and count it dearer than anything else. I cannot imagine people being fed up, it's glorious, and I somehow feel I am living in a sort of heaven at times which may be rudely shattered any minute. Ah! Well! At 11 A.M. I took a platoon and drilled it, trying to impart some of that spirit which is essential to those who would lay down their life for the "Good Cause." I drilled them for 1 hour and had them at the end of it fairly efficient as certainly they were the picture of efficiency at "presenting arms" both with bayonets fixed and unfixed. I then delivered [them] up to company formation when Major Hamilton inspected us.

The general had informed all our officers that Balaclava helmets were on no account to be worn by the men and that if they had no glengarry or Balmoral they must come out bareheaded.† At 12 P.M. we marched back. Edwards left to arrange about a pump so I dismissed the men on our parade ground right hand side of pond. Had lunch & found the "Eton Chronicle" waiting for me, also lists of Etonians on <u>Active</u> Service, Not <u>Home Defence</u>. The number up to January 30, though incomplete & inaccurate, is 1495, against 1494 who served in the South African campaign Oct. 11, 1899 to May 31st 1902.

So far	Killed in Action	=	179
	Missing	=	32
	Wounded	=	227
	Prisoners	=	18
	Wounded & Prisoners	=	32

The [true] number most probably is 2,000 as two fellows who I know have not got their names down.

---

* Jean-Baptiste Greuze (1725–1805) painted a series of moralizing portraits such as the one mentioned by Lionel. Although most of his pictures hang in the Louvre or the Wallace Collection in London, *Junges Mädchen* is still in the Kaiser Friedrich Museum in Berlin.

† The glengarry and the balmoral were both legitimate Scots caps, but the balaclava, which covered the head and shoulders, was used as a sleeping cap.

At 3 P.M. Edwards looked after cleaning up the billets and I took all the N.C.O.s, including the Company Sergeant Major, who accompanied to give them instruction in giving orders to their men, assembled on the same plot as we used in the morning. They were divided off Sergeants to one side, Corporals to the other. They then paired off & separated to about 30 paces distance & 100 paces internal between each man when he faced the other. They practiced shouting out their words of command to the man opposite, who performed the movement, and the man opposite yelled out the same orders in turn. Splendid practice for them. Because you may know the words of command & how to hold a rifle, but all that is useless if you are going to command men and cannot emit the sounds in the right way; for if the N.C.O. when drilling men, slurs over both words of command, then the men get lazy, & take no trouble, but if you are brisk and sing the first word out, so to speak, dragging it out, then pausing, & then cough at the next word, your men jump to it & carry the thing out with vim, eagerness and spirit unsurpassable. At least I find it so. The first word is the caution, the last is the command. I had to illustrate some of it but the men on the whole were excellent. Some had sore throats & some shouted the words out in piercing parrot cries, others in a way likened unto thin milk & others, the good, thick milk, so to speak. Milk, being only taken as a medium.

At 3 P.M. we returned & I to write letters, etc. I suppose I shall go to Mess in a few minutes, for believe me, it's now 7.15 P.M. I have been writing for almost 2½ hours.

∿

FEBRUARY 6 (SATURDAY) 7 P.M. A hard day's work. This poem which I found in the Eton College Chronicle is most catching.* Keeps coming up.

> I   We don't forget—while in this dark December
>   We sit in schoolrooms that you know so well
>   And hear the sounds that you so well remember
>   The clock, the hurrying feet, the chapel bell.
>   Others are sitting in the seats you sat in.
>   There's nothing else seems altered here—and yet
>   Through all of it, the same old Greek and Latin,
>   You know we don't forget.
>
> II   We don't forget you in the wintry weather

---

* *Eton College Chronicle*, 28 March 1915.

You man the trench or tramp the frozen snow;
We play the games we used to play together
in days of peace that seem so long ago:
But through it all, the shouting and the cheering,
Those other hosts in graver conflict met,
Those other sadder sounds your ears are hearing,
Be sure we don't forget.

III   And you, our brothers, who for all are praying
for this dear school of ours come back no more,
who lie, our country's debt of honour paying—
and not in vain—upon the Belgian shore
till that great day when at the throne in heaven
the books are opened and the Judgement set,
your lives for honour and for England given
the School will not forget.

And very nice, too. Eh! What! How I think of old Algy, only wish he was going to fight side by side with me.[*] A better fellow at heart never existed. A diamond uncut, but would look well with a good setting.

The magazine poem perhaps reminded Lionel of a poem of his own composition which he had written in a small notebook at Beuvry following the fierce fighting at Givenchy and La Bassée and which he now copied into his diary.

Poem for the heavy fighting Jan 24th to 25th
<u>many Etonians were killed</u>
<u>La Bassée</u>

I   The sky is clear with a very bright sun
Yet many dear lives are ebbing
The fellows we knew who with many a pun
In summer were with us out camping.

II   The time is changed, there's none can it doubt
And there's more to feel it soon
Yet out they'll come with hearts as stout
Just to become as cold as the moon.

---

[*] Algernon Belmont, a close Eton friend.

III	The trenches are wet and frozen with blood
	But all for one good cause.
	We stand up and fire with plenty of mud
	Adhering throughout every pause.
IV	Now there's one just here with a bullet wound
	Eton to him is no more
	Yet will he forget what there he booned?
	Why he's true, right down to the core.
V	The sky is darkening and many's the flash
	And many will dawn never see
	So good-by Old Eton, I'll yet have a dash
	For life's sweet as ever to me.

Aufwiedersehen

A pounding wet day and little doing. We dug trenches from 10 A.M. to 12 noon. The water came in as soon as we dug, so after completing 200 yards 3½ feet deep, we practiced getting in and out. Too slippery and of course too shallow. So we practiced on some trenches on the side of the hill. These I took a photograph of. In the afternoon we did fire control & fire discipline from the hill top. Have got a headache so will close for today.

5 Pills and Ills

7–11 February 1915

FEBRUARY 7 (SUNDAY) Woke up with an awful throat, feared it was a cold. 6.30 A.M. attended reveille & then men's breakfast. 9 A.M. parade for Church of Scotland. Roman Catholics paraded at 8.30 A.M. under the orderly officer. The colonel was present. His name is Stewart.* The original colonel was Duff. He was killed at the River Aisne. Then Major Murray took command until he was wounded in November. Col. Stewart then came on. As Major Hamilton is the senior colonel [major] here,† Major Murray has to take a company. "D" Company, very bad luck after commanding the battalion. Church parade was over by 9.45 A.M. I then rested as I was feeling shivery & cold & hot at the same time. Fear it's the flu. Now at 12 noon I went to the photographer 3 doors away and was photographed. One in my Burbury with Sam Browne belt on, and one in kilt, without apron. Mademoiselle Flore looked out of the window at the same time. She is a nice girl about 16½ or 17½ I should think. We are great friends and & get on well with our French. I try to teach her English and she in turn French. The old father wanted to photograph me with a "tableau" as he called it behind. I wasn't having any & told him his white-washed wall was much prettier to me.

At 1 P.M. I had lunch. At 2 P.M. I decided to go for a walk with Murdoch to see if it would not get rid of my nasty shiverings. We walked miles. Striking north we went through Lillers & then East towards Chocques. Retreating we returned through Lillers & struck west eventually reaching St. Hilaire 5 km distant from

---

* Lt. Col. C. E. Stewart replaced Lt. Col. Adrian Grant-Duff in command of the 1st Battalion in October 1914, and though wounded at 1st Ypres, he continued as commander of the battalion until January 1916, at which time he took over the 154th Brigade. He was killed by a stray shell later that year.

† Major J. G. H. Hamilton temporarily took over the battalion when Lt. Col. Stewart was sick in July 1915; he eventually took over the battalion permanently in January 1916.

Lillers, retreating our steps we returned to Lillers where, in a very old stationery shop I procured about 10 postcards. Some very old ones and which I shall always keep, one or two being placed in this book.

I felt very seedy coming back & feel rotten now, with a temperature I think. Well, I've stuck 6 weeks, ¾ awful weather & part in awful mud at Le Havre, and have been as fit as a fiddle the whole time seeing quantities going under with the flu & typhoid. At last I've got something I think. So good-night am off to bed without dinner.

Raining hard now with wind.

~

FEBRUARY 11 (THURSDAY) Four whole days in bed, the only ones spent there during my whole six months in the army. I am fairly well recovered now and may perhaps go out tomorrow so the doctor says but I am certain of it. To be in bed out here is rotten, nothing to do, and the exercise, which I like, with the ~~companied~~ Company denied me. I somehow don't think it's much good writing tonight as my thoughts are so loose. Have just written "companied" for Company (B). In order to remember events I will classify each day separately.

On Sunday evening I retired to rest about 5.30 P.M. Stubbs, our medical officer, came and saw me. He looked concerned and said I'd got a temperature which I think must have been fairly high, judging from the feeling of my body all over. Ever since then I have felt cooler every day, & every day he has said I've got a temperature even up till today when it is just above normal. Judging from his face & on the supposition that the feeling of my body gave practically identical results in proportion to its heat, that is to say, Oh, Goodness! I'm getting mixed up & cannot think. Well, if the foregoing sentence is intelligible to you, I work out on that formula as my basis that

> Thursday: temp was 97.5° Fahrenheit
> Wednesday: 98.5°
> Tuesday: 99.5°
> Monday: 100.5°
> Sunday: 101.5°

Thus you will see that my temperature might have been 101.5°, in fact anything from 100° to 103° though I think if we take the average, which is 101.5° F. we shall be fairly near it, & I did feel rotten too.

He sent me some pills, the smell of which caused me to reject, as they seemed not at all alien to me, and the results of which I had cause to regret more than once. That night I hardly slept at all but was in a comatose condition.

Next morning [Monday] I awoke very ill & was oblivious of most things all day except to sip some bovril* & to throw some pills & a filthy egg flip with brandy out the window. I slept well that night. Tuesday I felt a little better but an awful throat & very sore.

So now I find that I have to give my hot drinks, if they ever consist of any awful alcohol such as Rum or brandy, to my servant who shows an avidity none too pleasing. By the way my servant is none too good & since I have been in bed his faults have shown themselves much more, until I can scarcely say one good word for him. He is never punctual. He does not obey with alacrity. He is not smart or orderly in speaking & saluting which latter is his worst point. He is much too untidy, careless, & lackadaisical. He is also very skimpy and non-thorough in all that he does. I am most particular in having a clean room and everything in order, & his method is very jarring. Then again he is apparently very hard of hearing although only the other side of the door. He has, I am sure, delayed the progress of my throat, owing to the continual shouting & correcting his method. I now have my whistle and blow for him. Then again worst of all I miss things, match boxes & many small items. I found that he has used my writing paper, because when Richard was censoring some letters, he showed me two of Keekie's† and they were written on my yellow paper of a particular texture & fairly expensive which I bought in Le Havre, & of which I know he possesses none. However enough of his defects, if he would only ask for things first. However I am putting him into order, it being my first real opportunity, as lack of discipline in ranks, he has been out several months, has spoilt him. If there is no appreciable improvement within 1 week from now, back to his company he goes, for I shall be fed up like the chickens. There are, and it is only fair to narrate them, one or two good points about the fellow. Fairly cheering & not depressing, quick to recover his spirits & equilibrium, but useless to a certain extent in foraging.

~

FEBRUARY 10 (WEDNESDAY) Much better & doctor fairly cheerful. Very sleepy all day, so only drank some beef tea at 1 P.M. At 7 P.M. I was very

---

* A beef broth or beef tea.
† Lionel's servant.

hungry and the M.O. [medical officer] ordered an egg flip for me. No good as I knew so I sent my servant round to the mess to get me a special dinner:

soup
salmon (tinned)
preserved apricots (dried)
oatmeal biscuits & raisins
hot chocolate

He went to the head cook who doubted the good faith of the quest so interviewed the M.O. who cancelled my Ritz-like banquet for a bread & milk with rum. Ugh! No go. My servant lapped it up. Being really hungry, having had nothing but 1 cup of beef tea for lunch, Monday, Tuesday, & Wednesday, I sent my servant for some cakes & things from a shop in the village. He brought back a few. These I ate and had only just finished as Stubbs, the Medical Officer, came in. I was sent some gargle mixture which I was told being very poisonous was dangerous to swallow. Odd to be given so deadly a gargle, when if you gargle the wrong way, death may result, caused by the harmful properties of a certain medicine. Being no gargler & therein no wise skilled or practiced I deemed it safer to add about 12 Formalin tablets* to act as an antidote if any went down & also to give the stuff a better taste, also in that eventuality. I was then given two pills, of the brown & thoroughly evil German sausage type. Same being rejected by me were replaced by 2 very nice tasting flat tablets called Laxataf pills, destined for the same use, but of a nicer flavour, & not so volcanic. I also took 2 of the doctor's special sore throat cure tablets, 2 of the Formalin tablets, & 2 cubes of awful glycerine substances. All these diverse chemical products were taken in as I decided this was the great night, the last of all pills & ills & should therefore give one and all reliance to fight it out, and let the best one win. Well, as far as I can remember there must have been a battle royal of pills about 12 midnight, for I had a coughing fit, and I believe some few of the vanquished ones flew out by this emergency exit, to stop others coming out & shirking it as well as to stop the coughing I drank a glass of orangeade made that afternoon by me, and then took 2 more formalin pills who sailed downstream. Superior forces having arrived peace was restored as the Formalin pills must have killed all comers as no more fighting took place that night at any place along the line.

---

* The tablets produced a dilute solution of formaldehyde, which acted as an antiseptic.

FEBRUARY 11 (THURSDAY) Felt marvelously well and decided to write the journal in the evening. Visits were paid me by Major Hamilton (C.O. at present) and all the others including MacFarlane. I must here mention that Mademoiselle Flore continued to come every day when I was in bed & bring me Tisane [an herb tea], good for the throat. I did not like the smell, so always said "Pas boire encore" meaning "not drink yet." My servant did not like the drink as well, so I do not know what happened to it. As the visits were sometimes more than 3 times a day, I used to feign sleep & look the other way, as I got tired of talking with my throat and also considered one visit sufficient. Ah! My servant got it in the neck to-night. On entering the outer room I found all the dust laying about & a mess of paper on the floor & being tired of constantly finding fault, decided to give just one good blowing up, accordingly I gave it him, and he won't forget it as he is under threat of "being returned to duty" if no alteration is found soon.

They say that diphtheria has broken out in C Co'y now. Typhoid is already rampant everywhere. Yellow fever is also taking its toll. Dysentery in many and cholera in isolated cases. Besides which Flus galore are rolling round, so is not one better off in trenches where continually under the sky & shot & shell which things keep one's mind occupied, than in billets in a town or village herded together, nothing to think of except diseases, very nasty & unprepossessing thought. To be stricken down in the battlefield is much nicer than to be stricken down in billets with some awful disease. To die a glorious death is the former & to die a glorious death when dying for one's country, but at the same time a horrid one to fall foul of is the latter. One may & well say:

Typhoid to right of us
Old flu to left of us
Cholera on top of us
Diphtheria in front of us
Dysentery quite close to us
&
Yellow fever sitting at the very tip top
of us
with e'er a death around.

That's how the matter stands putting it in words and apart from enjoying the firing line I must say it is much more agreeable to me to be there, and meet death if need be in action than to fall foul of one of those horrors. I only wish the Germans would capture our infected, provided I'm not on the list, & so infect some of the sausage worshippers.

6 Mock Bombing Attacks

12–28 February 1915

FEBRUARY 12 (FRIDAY) Very cold day with snow on the ground. Still snowing and quite heavily at 9 A.M. when I considered myself fit for going on Parade. We had trench digging & bomb throwing etc. Edwards took two platoons to dig trenches while I took the other two and practiced them in bomb throwing & getting in and out of the trenches & charging out of a trench as quickly as possible. They then went on to platoon tactics & drill.

Bomb throwing

The bomb thrower must acquire a skill far greater than is judged by the ordinary soldier & perhaps cricketer, though the latter should be the best stuff for trying. In order to bomb throw with any success the most important thing is to see where you are going to throw it. Some men think their only object is to throw the thing away not troubling where it goes, chucking it away after the fashion of throwing away an old tin (as indeed it is). We have to use old tins about 4" high & 2 or 3" in diameter filled with earth. Thus, having read the above few paragraphs you will see that aim is everything, decidedly as a German is sapping in his trench & you must find him & plug the bomb where he is. Consequently before throwing your bomb you must bob up very quickly & take in all at a glance. This being done your target should have been ascertained. All's well, you throw your bomb, but how? Remember you are in 5 foot odd trench with a mound of earth in front perhaps & also behind. Also the trench is not wider, or should not be, than 2 ft. 6 in. because of the danger of shrapnel etc. Thus little room is given for the movement of limbs. Consequently much force must be put into the effort which finally let goes the bomb. Remember you must be very quick and not expose yourself because having bobbed previously may have told a German or a sniper that something is up.

So carefulness is needed. A very stiff, quick, & vigorous throw is necessary, & if both feet are firmly planted apart, impetus should be the net result. Success cannot at first be attained & much practice is necessary, though naturally throwing tins with earth & mud in them is difficult, whereas a bomb is rounder perhaps, heavier, & more adaptable for throwing. It must be remembered that the primary object of a bomb is not to cause wholesale destruction like a shell, but to get at men who owing to dugouts & carefully made trenches remain immune from rifle fire unless they show themselves. Also when sapping is going on, & mining, rifle fire will not touch the enemy, whereas a bomb, if it does not kill the enemy, will at least smash up his works perhaps. There is little more that I can think of about bomb-throwing and I only wish we had one or two crack bowlers, not in respect of adeptness in taking wickets but in having a strong knacky throw, which when fostered could be brought to a high pitch of excellence. However, we have one or two very good Minenwerfers, as the Germans call them, though a minenwerfer or mine thrower or bomb thrower sometimes means the mortar, which will throw a bomb, sometimes very large ones.

～

FEBRUARY 13 (SATURDAY) Hopelessly wet day all morning so we had a kit inspection. Many men showed the ravages of previous fighting for they were minus everything including their Pack, which before the charge No. 8 Platoon got orders to take off naturally. They lost them, for after the flush of victory little attention was paid to packs. In the afternoon the weather cleared somewhat and we had warm sunshine but treacherous. At 2.30 P.M. we took the "snipers" & bad shots down to the rudely constructed range, devised simply by having the bank of a large hill for the objects. The snipers did some good shooting and the bad shots some bad shooting as might be expected. Then about 4.30 P.M. when it was getting a trifle dusky a great rainstorm came on blotting out the landscape completely. Much wet & bedraggled we returned. I was orderly officer that night so had to collect the reports. Only 2 men absent.

～

FEBRUARY 14 (SUNDAY) Being Orderly Officer I have today, as it is Sunday, to take the Roman Catholics to church. Accordingly at 8.40 A.M. I went outside & found the men, an odd hundred, paraded & fallen in ready for me. Off we went and after 5 minutes arrived at Burbure Roman Catholic Church. I led them in, but finding a congregation crossing themselves & bowing, I thought something was wrong so order[ed] my men to "backwater." Once fairly going we slid out of the church backwards, but I am afraid we churned up the church by this motion as several men dropped their rifles on the flagstones. At last the people flocked out & the men flocked in. I was told [by] my Sergeant that all the officers who had brought the previous R.C. parades had attended the service so I went in too. As the service progressed I saw it would make a splendid photograph and as I took little interest in the service, I looked about for a good site. Having fixed on one I sauntered to the rear by some font place with water in it, resting my camera on this firm object. I took several interesting photos. They were "time" exposures. Unfortunately the click of the trigger as I pressed attracted some of the audience and as they were time exposures & not instantaneous when I could have covered it up quickly, I had to leave the camera in full view until the second click, when the photo would be taken; as this sometimes took 5 or 6 seconds naturally the audience at the back part, a few women who had remained or came in for the second sitting, had time to see the whole operation & looked askance. I was sorry for them & am sure looked it & the photos should be very good. To make sure of not forgetting, I unrolled the film there. This, I believe, shocked them still more, but I did not look up. As I did not use their holy water for sticking the gum paper, they were spared something to be grateful for. The service bored me frightfully & the German part toward the end was most exasperating. The clergyman, or whatever he's called, used to blow or ring some object like a bell. The audience would murmur some prayer, to be cut short by another blast, the absurd time idea for prayers is most German & should be abolished. For that reason if for none others, I shall henceforth be as strong pro-Catholic as I am now pro-German.[*]

As all this foolishness was drawing to a close a strong attack of urchins started. I suppose it was near the time for their service. They were tired of waiting outside I suppose. For some time past much talk had been going on outside the left door. At last laughs started & in they came. Red & white & greeny faced urchins with variegated scarves. Some went to my holy bowl (from which I had now removed my camera & retreated from) and others didn't, a great contrast in their religion. Some most devout in crossing, others careless. One young fellow about 8 brought in a younger one about 5. He seemed to be one who plays the fool, for he went to the bowl, took up water in both hands & practically swamped the young kid, there was much howling. He got ejected by the others & in the rush they fell over the rifles. This caused great confusion, and in the middle of it the congregation suddenly sprang to life and broke up. I must say, though not believing in the religion, that the men behaved in a far

---

[*] In other words, not at all.

more devout & quiet manner than do the men in church parades (Protestant). Indeed the whole worship seemed more devout. Of course, all this is part of the R.C.'s absurd ideas.

It started to rain when we got outside & when we got back developed into a deluge. There had been no church parade at 9.50 A.M. because of the rain. It rained all day. However I was determined to have some revolver practice in the afternoon, so having procured 30 rounds from the Quartermaster & another 30 of my own, leaving me now with 25, I had a good practice with 10 sets of 6 rounds each. The latter firings showed improvement over first at 30 yards range & much as that is necessary, at 10 yards range it was quite easy (and the object was large). Rain continued & lasted all day.

At 11 A.M. I should mention the Battalion barber, a member of C Company, cut my hair also nearly cutting my right ear off.

~

FEBRUARY 15 (MONDAY) Battalion Route march at 9.30 A.M. The previous night second Lieutenant Merrilees of the 4th Argylls whom I knew very well, and is slightly below me in superiority, joined us. He has been given No. 6 Platoon to look after. I have No. 6 Platoon when not helping Edwards in any other capacity. Accordingly we marched off so. We marched to a town Valhous, a small mining village southeast of Burbure & quite close to St. Pol, a distance according to the map of 13 kilometers out & 13 km back, a total distance of 26 kilometers. The march would have been much pleasanter if the road was not constructed of cobblestones. The country was most uninteresting, consisting mainly of coal mines and huge coal heaps & slag heaps on which anti-aircraft guns & other things are mounted. Indeed the country much resembles the black countryside round Birmingham except that it is cleaner. We returned about 1 P.M. having only had two halts the whole time. Our stretcher bearers and ammunition waggons accompanied us the whole way. Our flag bearer with the small & dirty flag, with 42nd inscribed on it, marched in front. In the afternoon Edwards sent me with half the Company to do shooting. I took them down to the so-called Butts & we started. I was doing the 15 rounds to be fired in 45 seconds. The Five succeeded in getting only 7 shots on, being the highest score, & 3 on, being the lowest.

~

FEBRUARY 16 (TUESDAY) In the morning we practiced a small scheme of attack. We attacked 2 lines of trenches, one above the other, the enemy fleeing to a small village beyond which we also gaily attacked. All worked out well as it should. We advanced over 1000 yards odd of perfectly flat ground with not the slightest cover & took at least half an hour to do it. No one laid down after he had done his rush, but stood up and gesticulated, being bored with someone else. Numbers 7 & 8 took the lead in extended order. I was the Supports & No. 5 Platoon was advancing up a sunken road, to be the reserve. I went on gaily, & did what those in front did, namely fix bayonets 100 yards from the enemy's trenches. Ten of my men were then asked for reinforcements to storm the trench. The man who brought the message had calmly sauntered whistling over the shot & shell racked ground, taking two minutes to come about 150 yards & the same time to go back. Just before the rush I ordered my men to rush up & reinforce. Edwards however, fearing my men were not coming had just ordered his men to advance, so my men suddenly found themselves left having just reinforced & come up 100 yards & being tired were done out of the charge not being able to go on. The attack was gallantly pressed on, the Reserve now coming up. Patrols were then sent in to disarm the inhabitants & take possession. Two & a half hours had been expended over the attack, we had to retreat. I must now add, the attack was merely done in the orthodox way, but quite impossible now. It showed the men how the trenches would be taken at the last, but the first part no one could have advanced over except by night or in a fog. Trenches would be there, & by sapping of course, we could have got near enough for a sudden assault, & then the main attack should have developed as we performed it. Perhaps all this was apparent to the men, & they realizing how impossible it would be to advance over the preliminary 100 yards, did not take the trouble of lying down & doing it so thoroughly as otherwise.

1st Black Watch
The Front
17. 2. 15

My dear Father,

Many thanks for your letter received today. I still have much of the chocolate you sent me & enjoy it very much.

What awful weather we are having. We are always wet although in billets. However it is better in comparison with that awful muddy camp, and soaking leaking tents at Le Havre. I look back at those three weeks with a shudder. I consider them worse by far than the trenches. Yesterday was beautiful, today is the awful ceaseless rain, we carry on tactics as usual. A great calamity has befallen us. We would think nothing of it in the trenches but here although only a couple of miles away it is rather grim. We practice bomb throwing here. Major Murray, our junior major already back from being wounded in Oct. was watching. Lance Sergeant Hart* of A Company took a bomb, bit the fuse and was waiting the usual 5 seconds before throwing it, when suddenly the fuse being defective burnt up quickly, and the bomb exploded. The man was in the trench. Major Murray, the Royal Engineer officer and some others were close by. The bomb blew one arm off, and most of the stomach, head and face. He was practically killed, but was supported by the sides of the trench. The explosion of the bomb set fire to his pouches and all his ammunition, about 150 rounds blew off, almost simultaneously. He received practically all these in him. Many bullets flew through him, and threw pieces of him yards away. He was quite dead now. Major Murray and the Engineer Officer and others received bullets. The Engineer officer received about 15 and is not likely to live. Major Murray received about 28, one passed through his eye and pierced his brain. It is believed he then became unconscious. He died that afternoon at 4 P.M., 5 hours later, very sad indeed, he was such a nice officer, though very strict and spent over half an hour talking to me when I was in bed with my throat etc. exactly a week ago I think. There was little left of Sergeant Hart, as pieces of him were picked up 20 yards away. His head resembled a slug-eaten and much-decayed cabbage. They picked up pieces of his stomach, and other parts, and he was together with these put into a bag and buried that afternoon.† All the Company present. Major Murray of D Company is being buried this afternoon at L_____ [Lillers].

   I have astonishingly little time to write now we are so busy. We were much worried by aeroplanes, more than 10 coming over. Some Germans were chased, and we saw quite 15 puffs break out below one, in the course of 5 minutes, it never came down however. At the lecture the other day General Haking‡ said that when we go back to the attack in a few weeks' time and K[itchener]'s Army is over, we are going to try a great advance, together with our new 17″ Naval guns, which can throw enormous masses I believe. We shall storm the enemy's trenches all along, and charge on to its second defenses, a line 15 miles back striking close to Brussels. A very costly job I expect.

Well goodby for the present
Your affectionate son,
Lionel Sotheby

[Diary resumes] 7 P.M. The orderly sergeant has just brought me orders. He says that Sergeant Hart, who was killed, was literally blown to pieces. The

---

* Sergeant P. Hart.
† Sgt. Hart's remains were buried in the Burbure cemetery.
‡ Major General R. C. B. Haking, commanding the 1st Division.

bomb blew one arm off & made a huge hole in the stomach, this, it is thought killed him. The cartridges in his pouches, about 120, blew his other arm off & most of his body & head & face. He says the other men collected quite a quantity of bits of him. The R.E. [Royal Engineer] officer is also not expected to live. Many other men were wounded.

Second Lieutenant McKenzie, Major Murray's one & only Subaltern, is to take the Company "D" at 1.10 P.M. tomorrow to Lillers 1st Field Hospital where Major Murray is at present lying. They will afterwards proceed to the funeral. The orderly sergeant was most upset. I liked Major Murray immensely, when I was ill he spent over half an hour speaking to me & also spoke to me this morning before his death.

∿

FEBRUARY 17 (WEDNESDAY) Hopelessly wet day so we gave lectures to the men. I lectured to No. 6 Platoon on trenches & also told them what General Haking said at the last lecture at headquarters last Sunday. I was not there but am told the substance of it was this: our Division, the 1st, will go into action again in the beginning or the middle of March. Most of Kitchener's army will be out by then. A preconcerted attack will then be made all along the line & we shall carry all the enemy's line of trenches. They then, we learn on good authority, have no more trenches for 15 miles, so we are supposed, I take it, to charge over this ground & dig ourselves in opposite this next line preparatory to taking it. By then we shall not be far off Brussels. We are to be assisted in all this by some enormous naval gun 17" or 22" which will fire 20 miles, & can hurl a projectile weighing 2 tons, which digs a hole 20 times larger than the Jack Johnson or Black Maria. Some gun I call it.

Well, I lectured to No. 6 Platoon on the trenches & then discoursed to them of General Haking's lecture & the powers of this wonderful gun, the powers of which some were doubtful of. On getting back to the mess I met Edwards who told me my platoon was waiting for the lecture. I told him I had just lectured. At length it transpired that I had been in command of the wrong platoon for a whole week. This comes of having to look after half the company so often while the other half does musketry with Edwards. Apparently No. 5 Platoon is the lawful one. This, I am told, is the "warlike Platoon." Why I do not know, but they like the name. Accordingly I went back & discoursed at length to this platoon as well. Since I have been in B Company besides being second in command and looking after a half company occasionally I have had the honour to be in command of No. 8 Platoon for 5 days, No. 6 Platoon for 8 days and now No. 5 Platoon forever more. Besides this while in D Company at Beuvry I was in command of No. 14 Platoon. At Béthune I was in command of No. 1 Platoon, A Company, and then for 3 days at Burbure here I had No. 2 Platoon, A Company. A good selection and variation, and yet all the time I was in the Argyll & Sutherland Highlanders I had No. 2 Platoon for 5 months odd. In the afternoon Major Murray was buried at Lillers. All D company marched there for the last rites. Edwards went too, so I had to look after the Company. Merrilees is in charge of No. 7 Platoon. He lectured and I lectured some of the N.C.O.s on the attack we did yesterday, its merits and demerits, also on Fire Control, and Fire discipline.

It persistently rained all day and was altogether most dreary. One important note, my servant is improving much, my belt is getting brighter & he cleans things up much better & his manner in general is much better. Discipline & plenty of it is working wonders.

~

FEBRUARY 18 (THURSDAY) A most beautiful day as it always is after 2 days' rain. It's always the same here. Today we are on trench digging. Edwards went on to look at the ground, so I brought the Company round. We found our old trenches flooded out, the water was actually level with the top & flowing over. One silly man went too close & slipped half in, luckily for him he did not go right in, as there was quite 5 ft 6 inches of water & then mud. We proceeded on & selected a new site 50 yards outside a wood. Merrilees set his platoon on to digging a trench some 100 yards long looking from the wood. No. 8 Platoon went into the wood & began digging a trench 50 yards long, about 10 yards back from the entrance. Some people do not like trenches on the edge of a wood like this because they say it draws shell fire, whereas the centre of the wood escapes. At least you can build one line of trenches on the edge & then have a communication trench back to the centre of the wood where your second trench could be. If it was too hot in the one, you could retire to the other. These two platoons being so engaged Edwards told me to go off & receive an attack of No. 6 Platoon. He looked after the trench digging. We were to be the Germans & were to keep up a running fight, while retiring through the wood about 150 yards wide. I happened to know the enemy consisted only of 28 men, & my strength being 34, I was able to use it to advantage. I drew them all up in one long line extended order from one side of the wood to the other, and awaited the attack with fixed bayonets. I had previously made a reconnaissance & found a little place surrounded with brambles. I decided to make a counterattack from this. Accordingly I gave orders that once we retired, No. 3 Section of 10 men, was to make for this place & await me, the others widening out & slipping by to our left under the command of my Sergeant. We waited among the scanty willow & nut trees interspersed with thicker elm trees, & having about 50 yards difficult field of fire. I sent a scout out who made an awful noise. At length Edwards, who by the way was heavily shot at by men, bravely came forward & said the British were advancing. He then went back, & my scout came back, who though late brought the same news. We saw the enemy yards away & fired at them, & should by right have annihilated them, yet these brave Britishers came on creeping from tree to tree, which by the way gave no shelter as a bullet would go right through. When the whole 28 were about 30 yards away, and each one of them must have received about 20 bullets in him we retired, the others gradually and I with my section to our redoubt. They did not see us as we were to the other side of a small rise in the ground. We crouched down out of sight & saw our men go past. Then two minutes later the enemy came, one man walking right on top of us. We captured him & suddenly from our place poured a withering fire into the flanks of the enemy. If not annihilated before, no one could have lasted this last, for we then charged & took 8 prisoners. The enemy fell back a little to recover their dead, presumably, & we retreated with our prisoners to a small disused cottage by the side of the wood. I then tried my last ruse. The enemy had only 21 men now, 9 being captured.[*] I left one on guard over them, well away from the field of operations, & prepared my last attack. I allowed 10 to keep up the extended order retirement, & take up a strong position behind a bank on the outskirts of the wood, I with my other 24 men, superior to the enemy's 21, most of whom should be either wounded or killed, mine should not, as we had better cover & did not have to expose ourselves as they did advancing, went round the wood single file & lay in a pit, until my scout told me the enemy were past us in the wood. We then sallied out & in extended order came up behind the enemy firing hard & doing a great charge, thus hopelessly enfiladed they should have been smashed utterly but by so thinking one utterly underrates the British. They, brave men, already killed 5 times over turned round & though assailed 1½ to each of our men put up a stubborn fight, and declared themselves victors until even their sergeant said he thought we had won & they had been the losers. The men enjoyed this attack immensely, saying it was the best bit of fun they had had yet. We then

---

[*] Either Lionel's arithmetic was poor, or more men remained in the "enemy" platoon than he thought.

returned to the digging area & relieved the other Platoons, who after a rest, went through more or less the same operations.

I took my Platoon No. 5 to the digging in the wood, and after exhortations & digging myself for 10 minutes, which is the best way to get the men working, the work went on apace. We struck many roots & the water started coming in up at the Northern end, so I gave instructions for a sunk pit 10 feet deep & 4 feet wide to be dug 2 yards to the rear of the trench with a small drain or communication trench leading back. Stones we then got ready to put at the bottom as a drain. By 3 P.M. we had finished the trench & filled it with a great quantity of stones found in the soil for drainage purposes. I then had some of the thin brush wood cut down from the front. Meanwhile a dugout had been built at the back communicated by a short trench of 5 yards from the main one. I had three fairly large trees (30 feet high) felled by means of our very sharp bill hooks. Thus we got some supports & cross pieces. Branches intertwined formed the roof. Brushwood was interlaced & piled on top again & earth thrown on top. Brushwood was put on the floor inside & the dugout was fairly completed. It was capable of holding about 10 men. At 4.15 P.M. we knocked off. Edwards liked the trench but was afraid the C.O. would not like the trees being cut down. However I am content, if a thing's worth doing it's worth doing well & no trench is complete without its dugout.

~

FEBRUARY 19 (FRIDAY) No post today. Rumour has it that the Packet boat was sunk with our letters, some of the men in B Company got quite angry when they heard it. Rumours are coming through that the Germans are blockading us in real earnest, but it's probably all bunkum. One thing, however, the men in this regiment are in wonderfully good spirits now, indeed the singing and the whistling on the march today proved they are fit for anything and are not at all fed up, though some may grouse and create a bad impression on the pessimist who immediately thinks the whole army is fed [up] and of no more use as a fighting force. The men are in splendid condition & fit for anything at any time.

~

FEBRUARY 21 (SUNDAY) A beautiful fine day all day. Roman Catholics had their service at 8.50 A.M., we paraded for Church of Scotland at 9.30 A.M. At 10.50 A.M. Merrilees took the Church of England parade. In the afternoon the London Scottish officers came over & played us at a soccer match. They were a very brawny lot & had a few really good soccer players among them. The result although humiliating was by no means astonishing. They beat us 4 goals to nothing. On our side Merrilees was the best at "right back." It was a beautiful afternoon and thoroughly adaptable for the game. The men were most enthusiastic, cheering lustily & with great vigour.

Lieutenant Lord Hay has just turned up.* He was wounded and has now just come back bringing a draft of 67 men. They have just posted them to the Companies now. We have 17 posted to our Company. Hay is an immense fellow being just over 6 foot 11 inches, practically 7 feet high. He simply towers over everyone. Indeed at first on coming out of my dwelling I thought a lamppost had suddenly been erected till he turned round.

~

FEBRUARY 22 (MONDAY) A very cold day indeed with a severe frost. The previous night had been moonlit and beautiful with its ceiling of stars and planets. A thick & cold fog overhung everything. Edwards stayed behind for Orderly Room. So I went with Hay, who by the way is in "B" Co'y, it being his old Company. Not knowing the way to the digging ground I led the way. I found our trenches in the wood had been filled in because the owner said we had cut the roots of his trees and they would die. Also by the way he has sent in a bill for £3 for the wood I cut down for the dugout. Such awful unpatriotism I have never met before. The colonel knows about it, so some arrangement may be come to. The wood if chopped up & sold at a penny a lump as in England would certainly not have fetched more than 10/, & he wants £3 Not having any.

Here's another instance of unpatriotism. In one of the billets a soldier was climbing about in the attic, which was his quarters. Suddenly owing to the house being very loosely and slackly put together, a tile or some object, being unsealed fell into the good lady's bread-tub at which she was industriously working. The object smashed part of the tub & also squirted some bready substance into her face & onto her clothes. She has sent in a bill to Edwards for 50 francs! (£2) Oh! the French are a funny lot, it takes a lot to understand them.

We finished our main trench 150 yards long, dug two communication trenches 70 yards back, & dug another uncompleted 150 yards' trench. We also drove a mine, tunneling 15 yards, 6 feet below the surface. This mine will be continued

---

* Lt. Lord F. Hay, wounded 22 October 1914 at Ypres and again at Loos 25 September 1915, was reputed to be the tallest soldier in the British Army.

next digging day. It is intended to tunnel 300 yards to the enemy's trenches which are to be blown up.

We also did some sapping, that is to say, one has to dig a trench with the various angles towards the enemy, but you have to keep under cover the whole time. Perhaps you will throw out 3 saps. On getting 100 yards out they will then link up & you have your trench 100 yards nearer the enemy. The idea in sapping is you must keep out of sight & yet dig forward, it is a very difficult undertaking. Sometimes you merely sap forward to get near enough to the enemy's trenches to throw a bomb—if your trench is a little too far off—you throw it from here.

In the afternoon we continued digging and really when we stopped at 4.30 P.M. we had had enough of it. 3 hours in the morning, 2½ hours in the afternoon. By the time we finished we [had] driven our mine about 6 yards towards the opposing trenches. At 3 P.M. the fog came down still lower and an awful rain drenched us. However we stuck to it for 1½ hours longer. Those in the tunnel were quite dry, as they had got down about 10 feet & were working in yellow sandstone, making great headway. On returning we ran into an enormous funeral about 300 yards long & almost 200 people attending. Judging from the size of the coffin one would almost expect that 3 families of 6 each had been therein deposited. Certainly the queue which formed up in column of route outside the village church must have consisted of 6 families. Where they bury the unfortunates I do not know, as the place has neither church yard or cemetery. They are all Roman Catholic in religion, so perhaps they are burnt. There sometimes is a nasty smell about the church & village. A funeral goes by every day, at least it has for the last 2 weeks for we were greeted with a funeral on our arrival. The death rate is something awful. Babies seem the chief unlucky ones. Our M.O. told me he considered the French doctor not first class, certainly his patients get off his hands quickly. 16 deaths have been reported in the upper part of the village since our arrival. What the lower part & distinctly the larger half contributes I do not know. The death statistics of this village would prove very interesting to examine.

Description as once witnessed: A town crier or some one marches in front of the advance party of small kids or girls bearing wreaths, crosses & the usual paraphernalia. Next follows a decrepit old man dressed in pink. He does not always appear, sometimes being late for parade I suppose when the procession has formed up. The priest then follows, always with an enigmatic and profound semblance of a sardonic smile on his accusatory and highly objectionable countenance. Then follows usually pitiful to behold the hired mourners for no parade is considered chic & finished unless it has some people to mourn in case the others do not feel up to it not being in good form, as they are rather glad of the departure that otherwise indeed perhaps they have hastened it, who can tell, and some French are very inhumane though it is rare.

∽

FEBRUARY 23 (TUESDAY) We dug trenches in the afternoon and made our older ones more perfect. We also drove our 3 sapping trenches forward 15 yards. The mine was tunneled forward to nearly 20 yards from the entrance. We broke off work at 4.30 P.M. being drenched through with rain for the second time that day, or rather the 4th time.

Shand (2/Lieut) came back in the evening and Captain Fortune our adjutant,* who has just been made a Brevet Major, also returned from leave. Several messages of excitable news from the front arrived during the evening. We are ready to go off at ½ hour's notice, and is firmly believed we shall be gone by Monday the 1st of March, or anyhow by the end of next week, March 7th. Heavy rain is now falling, but looks like clearing and being a frosty night, as it's getting abominably cold already.

∽

FEBRUARY 24 (WEDNESDAY) What an awful day. Snow & fearful blinding snowstorms "der ganze tag" (the whole day). Very cold indeed. Towards nightfall the temperature went down a little, the snow melted slightly. Will probably freeze again tonight. Bombardment still continues 7.30 P.M. In the afternoon the Battalion was suddenly called out with ambulance, transport, field kitchens, machine guns, pack horses in attendance. It was a false alarm, & after waiting 1½ hours in a blinding snowstorm we were dismissed. We thought we were off to the trenches as we are under half hourly notice to go off.

Haldane was out all morning instructing some men in bomb-throwing. Over 30 bombs were thrown & no one was blown up. I quite expected not seeing Haldane again. It's getting very cold again now & looks as if it's going to freeze tonight.

Our old Machine Gun officer has now returned,† so I don't know what will happen to MacFarlane. The bombarding still continues; there must be an attack on.

---

* Capt. V. M. Fortune.

† Captain F. G. Chalmer, wounded 26 October 1914 at the Second Battle of Ypres, was later transferred to the 3rd (Special Reserve) Training Battalion.

FEBRUARY 25 (THURSDAY) There was a great snowstorm in the morning, and the snow was quite deep, but swept away a bit.

Parade was ordered for 10.10 A.M. when the pipes would play. 10.15 the General would arrive.

I arranged with my photographer to have us photoed also to try and get one of the General. I told him he must do it from his bedroom or doorway, as if seen in too conspicuous a position he might get arrested or shot. He promised to comply. At 9.30 A.M. I journeyed down to my platoon parade ground, the snow was rotten & it was bitterly cold. Suddenly as if by magic the snow ceased & the sun blazed out from an azure sky. Never have I seen such a beautiful sky with snow underneath except in Germany last February. It was I should think a typical Alpine day. The sun was immensely warm & the snow began to melt at an astonishing speed.

Suddenly at 10.15 A.M. the guard in front of the Mess turned out, & we knew the General was approaching. Captain gave the "present arms" & all officers saluted. The pipers playing about 2 lines of the usual tune played for such big nuts. I forget the name of it, I did see it in orders. When the General came the Battalion was formed up in the order as depicted. He inspected us going along each platoon in turn. At the finish 10.38 A.M. he came forward in the snow & made a speech. Curiously enough he merely dwelt on the doings of the regiment & it struck me that he was trying to touch on things that would stir us to great fighting. His speech was modelled and harped entirely on the one theme.

After the usual formula of saying he was very pleased to have seen us and to have found the regiment turned out so well, he dwelt on its doings. He pointed out that it was the premier regiment of Scotland, the Royal Highlanders, or as better known "the Black Watch," and that being so, the regiment would naturally be expected to do great things by Scotland. He said its traditions in the past were as good as any other boast, and that the recent fighting on the Aisne, Marne, & at Ypres and La Bassée proved it still had the old fighting qualities which had made it so renowned a regiment. He then went on to say that he was sure the spirit which had animated recently still animated them now and would carry them on to victory glory, gaining even still greater honour. He ended "And now I will leave you," a few words I shall never forget.

It was General Haking who delivered himself of this address. He was attended by another General and 15 of his Staff, including 2 Brigadiers and 2 Brigade

Majors. And wonderful to say, the gay assemblage of stars was being photographed only 30 yards away in country a few miles behind the firing line where cameras are forbidden.

At 10.50 the General left. All during this time the sun's heat had been very powerful, indeed one man fainted although I doubt from heat. The glare thrown up from the snow was very trying to the eyes. However it was melting fast, and had turned into a muddy slush, where we had tramped about.

As it was 11 o'clock before we were dismissed, the order was given out to clean billets, so that occupied the men for the remainder of the morning.

Towards 12.30 P.M. the sun seemed to lose its power a great deal and it began to freeze in the shade, making things very slippery and dangerous. In the afternoon we threw bombs and did several attacks on trenches. First the bomb throwers rush forward throwing bombs at the enemy—intermingled with them are men with fixed bayonets to finish off those killed by the bombs & to occupy the trench. These again are quickly followed by the sappers who on reaching the trench hurriedly throw the parapet across to the other side in order to face the Germans. Meanwhile the support comes up to fill up casualties. A very beautiful day and the nicest I have ever known in this sunless country. Rumours go we are off to the trenches tomorrow, but nothing is certain, with German spies about.

~

FEBRUARY 26 (FRIDAY) Very cold indeed & thick ice everywhere. We did another attack in the morning. Hay took platoons and performed a rear-guard action through the village retiring on to the old wood we have fought in so much. We had to drive him out of the village, as some of his men had remained in yards and outhouses to snipe at us. These were captured & we advanced on the wood, going right through it & clearing it of the enemy. We attacked them finally & dispersed them. Returning Hay and I did the attacking. We made a plan. Hay was to go to the right side of the wood & to take a flank attack, & we would go easy to keep the enemy by a farmhouse. We heard the signal advanced as he did. Result two sections of the enemy were captured by the farmhouse. They vigorously protested saying that they had two machine guns & could have mown us down. They pointed to two knife grinders. Anyone can say they have machine guns, if they only have a grindstone to show, the statement doesn't hold water. However we had overlooked the barn & I saw a rifle pointed out of it. We caught the fellow, a sniper who said that he had shot the lot of us. I argued saying that if he had been shooting with live cartridges we should have heard him & surrounded the barn. Also he could not snipe, when prisoners and men were standing together.

We were told at lunch that we leave tomorrow for the trenches, to the left of Béthune & La Bassée. Also that the French were sending 50,000 men to help the Servians [Serbians] & we were sending 2 Divisions of Yeomanry against the Hungarians in alliance with the Servians. Also many ambulances had been brought up to the firing line by the French & huge reinforcements. Looks like a great attack. By the way we were also told that the war would be over by August, which I don't believe for a minute. Next January will be more likely. By 2 P.M. most of the snow had melted and it was quite warm. The day has been simply glorious not a cloud visible all day & a perfect azure sky.

We were informed, also, at lunch today that we leave tomorrow afternoon. This news was ratified later, when we were told the Battalion would move off at 1 P.M. & travel to Hinges, where we should billet for the night. Probably at 3 A.M. next day, though time is not stated, we shall move on again. Our objective is Festuberg [Festubert] by the firing line, E.N.E. of Béthune & W.N.W. of La Bassée about 6 km from Béthune & 4 km from La Bassée. The march there is about 18 km by the round about way we shall go, the journey to Hinges being between 11 km. & 12 km. Festubert is on the Givenchy & Cuinchy line, and they say the object in sending us there is to take some trenches of the enemy that have remained immune from attack for ages.

From all accounts our great offensive in alliance with the French is about to come off, & perhaps they are waiting for the 1st Division to come up after their rest.

It is very easy for people in England to say when is the offensive coming off and all that, but let them come out here & see the difficulties & put themselves in General French's place, & see the awful responsibility of advancing too soon, when your army may be too small & you find the Germans too large when you advance, but not till then. A rout may follow who can tell.

Both sides realize that issues at stake are the greatest of the war, & so it is little wonder that the Generals on either side are waiting, but it can hardly be compared to the famous "Wait & See" policy, as both sides are waiting mainly for reinforcements & good weather. It is not marking time, but "strategy," a totally different word. According to General Haking our first advance is only going to be 15 miles, but on the other hand all along the line. So that the first attack should take the line.

In the afternoon I had to fill in some trenches which had water to the top. We attempted to drain it off; but it was useless. Result was that we had much earth over & the trench was so squashy that you sank up to your knees straightway if you stood on it. In a week's time it will have sunk about a foot I expect. But that doesn't matter in the least.

~

FEBRUARY 27 (SATURDAY) Awful snowy day and very cold indeed. The orders were: Platoon commanders inspect billets at 10.30 A.M. see everything left clean. 11 A.M. Company commanders inspection to see everything finally cleaned up. 12 noon dinner. 12.30 P.M. Platoons parade. 12.45 P.M. Companies parade. 1 P.M. Battalion marches off. Before going further I must mention that I had to perform a most awkward thing. My servant Thursday got into trouble in the village & got punished. Other people were also bored with him, and as I had occasion to speak to him before, he had to go. He was very much loathe to, however, & I had much difficulty in his going as his nature is so odd. I now have a capital servant Jamieson whom I feel I can trust. We made an inventory of all I possessed in the morning which I got him to sign. Thus I know what I have got now. Alas I find I have lost many things. My pipe, one I bought in Berlin last January & a good smoker, has disappeared, also my light trench waterproof sheet which was very handy owing to its weight. I believe Keekie, my ex-servant pawned it in the village, as well as several other things I now miss. Unluckily time has always been against me to examine things before, & after all one can get worse servants than my last. Other people have found so. Jamieson is however highly satisfactory at present. I am much disconsolate about the pipe as I have 3 pounds of tobacco & the wherewithal to use it is absent.

Many people have been sending me medicine including Mother. Up to date I have

> 4 bottles of formalin pills
> 1 box of quinine pills
> 1 box of chest pastilles*
> 2 boxes of laxative pills
> 1 box of Tamar Indian†
> 1 box of cough lozenges
> 3 boxes of meat lozenges‡
> 1 bottle of frostbite mixture

---

* Aromatic lozenges.
† Tamarind, an herbal medicine.
‡ Tablets of meat concentrate.

1 bottle of liquid lice killer
1 bottle of disinfectant
4 oxo cubes*
3 Bovril tins
& last one bottle of morphine pills, one [pill] for semi-conscious-
ness, which has the effect, when being wounded, of making you
not mind anything, in fact laughing grotesquely at a German if he
wants to finish you off with a bayonet. Four pills however end you.
These I bought at Southampton.

At 11.30 A.M. I went to my photographer & asked for the bill of sundries,
developing, etc. 40 francs 50 centimes was the order. An awful cheat it seems to
me and another instance of the awful unpatriotic sentiment which pervades the
people of this village. I am certain 15 francs would have been the proper price.
I cannot talk French well enough to argue, and as any "half-paying" would be
bad form & cause dissatisfaction & give us perhaps a bad name, the sum was
paid. Meanwhile an awful snowstorm with a mixture of sleet & rain was raging.
We marched off at 1 P.M., our regiment, transport and all was ½ a mile long.
When crossing exposed country we caught the full force of the snow & sleet
sideways. An awful wind was blowing & hail now & then stung one up horribly.
The colonel was not with us having gone over to see the country in a car. We
passed through Allouagne where the Sussex regiment were stationed. They are
in the second Brigade & follow us tomorrow. The third Brigade follow the next
day, thus the 3 brigades (the 1st Division) will or should all be up by Tuesday.

Well passing through Allouagne where a football match was in progress, we
reached the railway bridge, under which you pass before coming into the main
road Lillers, Chocques, & Béthune & La Bassée, a cobbled one too. We fell out
here & waited 1 hour in the awful conditions of snow & cold. Meanwhile the
Scots Guards were at our rear & had formed up in Mass in a field.

The whole Brigade was going to march up, that is the 5 Battalions, 1st Coldstream Guards leading, then the London Scottish Territorials, then the Camerons (1st), then we, & last the 1st Scots Guards. Our whole length was 2½
miles. Each regiment was ½ a mile long.

We passed through Chocques where the brigadier was standing by the side of
the road to inspect us. "Eyes right" was of course given. Owing to the corners
much blocking took place causing delay & then everyone hurried to fill up the

---

* Oxo was a brand of bullion cube that made a nutritious hot drink.

gaps. We passed through Chocques & passing some aeroplane tents we saw the road 3 miles away winding round a hill. We must have lost about ½ a mile between the regiments in the march because we could see the head of the column twisting round the far corner. The London Scottish had lost nearly a quarter of a mile. The road here was very bad & carts were constantly getting rutted up. We passed 3 up to their axles in mud. There were constant stoppages on the march due to this, and standing about in the bitter cold & rain as it now was, was no joke. At the bottom of the hill leading into Hinges there was a long halt, the delay was due to billeting ahead which was in progress. Also two London Scottish transports had stuck deep in mud and were unmanageable. All the blankets had been thrown out of one but when we passed it, it still would not move.

Well we marched right through Hinges, passing the London Scottish, billeted in the lower reaches & the Camerons in the upper reaches. The Coldstreams we did not see. The Scots Guards turned to right some way before reaching Hinges, & went into Billets there.

We still marched on right through Hinges and looked as if we were for the firing line that night, but it was not so. Soon we crossed the La Bassée canal which was all fortified & ramparted & barbed wired. Passing on we at last came to Choquaux, part of Locon, N.N.E. of Béthune. Here we billeted arriving at 6.45 P.M. having been on the march for about 5¾ hours & travelling about 18 kilometers. Our route was most round about.

It took us a whole hour arranging the whole of B Co'y in the outbuildings of a farmhouse our billets were further on. After settling the billeting, we examined our billets. Four of us, Edwards, Hay, myself, & Merrilees were all in one small room 12 feet long & 8 feet wide. Edwards had a bed.

At 8.30 P.M. we went to the Mess where we got something to eat. The Mess servants had gone on ahead to arrange things.

The colonel was there & we were told the Battalion was to go into the trenches at darkness on the morrow. They were at present held by the Indians (the Gurkhas) & were reported in a filthy condition. Typhoid being much in evidence.

B Company was to hold some trenches only 110 yards from the Germans and were to throw bombs at the Germans every night at different times.

Being so informed I retired to bed, which looked very inviting, as my equipped [equipment] rubbed me sore in several places.

The exact equipment was:

Webb equipment, consisting of
  Shoulder strap & pouches
  Haversack (on left side)
  Water bottle (right side)
  Entrenching blade & holder (at back)
Extras:
  Field glasses in case
  Revolver (Webley) loaded & ammunition
  Rucksack on back
In haversack were the following:
  Electric torch & 1 battery
  Morphia pills, chest pastilles, Formalin lozenges, meat lozenges &
    bovril
  2 handkerchiefs
  2 slabs of Potin Chocolate
  6 films (camera)
  2 candles
  Camera
  1 pair of mitts
  1 pair of socks
In the neck-sack there were:
  4 pairs of socks
  4 pairs of handkerchiefs
  1 Cardigan jacket
  2 mufflers
  1 Balaclava helmet
  1 waterproof (to slip over)
  8 candles
  hair brushes & shaving kit
  Diary & notebook
  Writing case
  Tobacco
  14 films for camera
  Canteen
  Knife, fork & spoon
  1 Reschau du Soldat
  2 boxes of matches
  1 small saucepan

1 pr of mitts
Frostbite lotion & more lozenges

This weighed a little, & being unused to it our march was a bit heavy.

~

FEBRUARY 28 (SUNDAY) It is now 12 noon. We have definite orders to march off at 3 P.M. By 5 P.M. we shall have arrived near Richebourg l'Avone (not Festubert) near where are the trenches.

They say there are no communication trenches & that getting in is very dangerous. Relief & food cannot come by night. By 6 P.M. we should be amongst the filth & water. What a glorious life. Little do people in England realize what it is like to feel that you are about to go into trenches for a month that evening and that it is a hundred to one against your escaping some wound during that time. No, nobody who has not done it realizes what it is. However keen you are, even as I am, one wonders for a moment & thinks what will happen. However I am enjoying myself immensely.

I got up 8 A.M., walked to the mess & had breakfast. Then walked to the men's billets and saw everything was in order. The sun was now shining brilliantly and walking to the N.E. of Choquaux surveyed the scene. In front were trenches 20 yards off, a defensive line for Choquaux, in front of these again were barbed wire entanglements. I photographed them all. Before proceeding further I should say the land here is ploughland & absolutely as flat as a table. You can see four miles at least & much further were it not for scattered trees. The soil is not clay, but loamy soil, with the water laying about on the surface. Consequently the walls of the trenches will not stand up & have fallen, & the water is nearly level with the top. Two dugouts dug to the rear & with huge stanchions have fallen right in as the banks have given way. There is no clay on the surface but there is 5 feet down and this keeps the water from flowing away. I took photographs of all & afterwards photographed my servant Jamieson, Edwards' servant & Merrilees' servant also Haldane himself. The day was perfectly clear. Béthune Church stood up very clear as it is quite 200 feet high I should think. Beuvry church stood up to the left & Locon church only 500 yards away in the trees.

Well I don't know when next I shall write my diary.

7 Into the Trenches for the First Time

28 February–6 March 1915

We have had a time of it. There's no time to go into details. We marched up & got into the trenches somehow, without any casualties. The trenches are really breastworks with no back cover whatever & very dangerous for shell or bomb fire. My Platoon was in an old blown-to-pieces barn or house 300 yards behind our breastworks & getting up to the breastworks from there was very dangerous owing to snipers; unless you bent double you were seen.

One had also to pass through a ruined farm which had no communication trench & used to get shelled continually, as the Germans always saw us crossing there. Our breastworks are after the fashion of redoubts & very easy to take I should think.

Cannot write more, so will only give headings which may let me improve upon later when we are resting.

～

FEBRUARY 28 (SUNDAY) 3 times to ramparts. Much sniping several wounded. 5 snipers on door close shave of 5 bullets on the roof while observing. Dead cattle. Photographing. Discovery of 5 dead Gurkhas in trench. A well full of them. Awful stomachaches & upset. Very cheerful & content. Everything most interesting. Same night alarm 11 P.M. turn out. Return 12 midnight in ramparts till 7 P.M. next evening.

～

MARCH 1 (MONDAY) Merrilees sick but full of go. Cold night. Much sniping. Heavy cannonade towards Ypres at 3.30 A.M. Morning beautiful.

MARCH 2 (TUESDAY) Several photographs. Our support house 300 yards back got 15 to 30 shells, also the ruins. Dead cow blown to bits awful smell. Cannonade both sides & great shellfire on farms. Periscope very useful. Could see German rampart blown in by 5 shells at 2 P.M. 100 yards away. 3 P.M. Support House again shelled about 15 shells, Minenwerfer suspected. 5 Mortars to be brought to our trench for night. Platoon undamaged. Several men altogether killed or wounded. Merrilees sniped some Germans, I improved on a rotten dugout. 7 P.M. relieved by Coldstream Guards. South Staffs & H.L.I. [Highland Light Infantry] lost one of trenches sometime back. Sniping very fierce. Went to some billets ½ mile back got to bed 12 at night [Tuesday night] was outside 4 times in night, diarrhoea. No sleep. Tremendous cannonade & attack at Givenchy.

March 2, 1915

My dear Mother,

We came out last night after having had an awful 48 hours in breast-works. Just here there are no trenches, but breastworks of sandbags. They are not continuous, are built like redoubts, consequently you get fierce fights when attacks are made. We got no sleep, as orders to go visiting redoubts. Between them you have to dash as all snipers and good shots of the Germans range on them. We got it beastly yesterday and they blew in some breastwork and shelled our supports stationed in a smashed up farm house 300 to 400 yards back by an orchard. It had about 50 shells and a mine was got under it. Awfully lucky escape they had as the first did little damage and warned them. They rushed out and the place was blown up. My platoon was 50 men, but I was ordered up to the firing breastwork 5 minutes before the first shell came. The place is littered with dead horses and cattle. One shell burst on one and blew it to pieces, the smell is awful and I had [only] to smell my mackintosh to get rid of it. I have awful diarrhoea and when one goes behind the breast-work the snipers fire at you, it's awful. My stomach feels out of existence, but for that I am enjoying myself immensely. The periscope is very useful, through it I saw 5 of our shells blow up 20 yards of German breastwork 150 yards off, 4 Germans lay outside. Quite 60 shells fell on their support house 400 yards back. I feel very tired and we came out after 48 hours and go in after a day's rest. We have six weeks of it unless the regiment get out. Must end now as I am frightfully tired. Our casualties are about 30 so far. Cannot write further yet. No cigarettes yet, much needed. Also [send] 1 pipe & cake. Sometimes food does not come up.

Your affectionate Son
Lionel

MARCH 3 (WEDNESDAY) [Diary resumes] 5.30 A.M. Thought we would be called out, busy all day. Much shelling during day. Jamieson, my servant's narrow escape from shell, covered with mud, rifle damaged. Afraid shell would fall on our house. 200 men in barn too dangerous if shelled. Losses. 4.30 P.M. moved ½ mile further away passing the R.F.A.[Royal Field Artillery]'s graves on left over 400 of them. Must take photo sometime. Billets bad for men, my platoon got worst. 7 P.M. ordered with Hay & 200 men to go digging all night. Went to firing line & dug ramparts. Sniped all time. Many stray shots. One sapper shot through head sideways, as we were enfiladed. Beastly rain & cold later. Filthy mess. Men worked well. Finished 2.30 A.M. [Thursday March 4]. London Scottish helped, returned 3 A.M. Soaked, got 5 hours sleep very chilly & damp. Waterproof sheet also soaked from my coat in morning. Very tired. Went round platoon 9 A.M.

March 4, 1915

My Dear Mother,

 Up all last night with 200 men digging and making a breastwork of sandbags etc. 300 yards from the Germans. We were shot at the whole time. One of our fellows was killed. It poured with rain and we got back at 4 A.M. (from 7 P.M.) soaked with rain but exceedingly cheerful. The only thing was the awful stomachaches and diarrhoea which empty me every 10 minutes and make me feel exceedingly weak. However the bullets have quite an exhilarating effect on me, keeping my spirits up and the shells are quite interesting to watch burst when they are more than 30 yards away. We go into the breastworks again tonight at 7 P.M. Since Friday night I have had a bare two hours sleep, but I assure you it's much better than Sunderland because you are so interested and never know what's going to happen next. Sunderland was monotonously dull.

 We relieved the Gurkhas and they, filthy things, buried all their dead 3 feet back from the breastworks and we are constantly putting our spades through half decomposed black bodies. One well is full up with them. Our old support house 200 yards back got another 30 shells yesterday, they tell us. The back is simply littered with graves of the S. Staffs and H.L.I.

 My servant was nearly killed yesterday, a shell burst 10 yards from him, when walking on a road and covered him with mud, smashing his rifle in. He was going to send my last letter to you, and was on the way from the line.

 Well I must end now, as am awfully tired, and can barely see the paper. Our casualties are about 30 or so I think. Do send cigarettes, cake, & things as dates etc. sometimes as rations do not come always, & one gets hungry, others also appreciate.

P.S. Don't think I am at all fed up, because I am enjoying myself, (if only my stomach gets right) I think it's bending in the breastworks.

We go to trenches again tonight at 7 P.M. to relieve Coldstreams. We take over A Company's old trench.

Your affectionate Son
Lionel

MARCH 4 (THURSDAY) [Diary resumes] There were no dugouts so conditions were rotten. It rained too, the whole 48 hours, which prevented me from taking any photographs. The men as usual were excellent in every way, & that was they were too careless. Continual growling from me at last showed improvement. We got one very annoying shelling one day from a small gun or two, but really it was nothing to inspire dread, & bullets afterwards are as nothing. Today I lost Corpl. Gibb of my platoon. He was a good man & trustworthy. Poor fellow. Got his cheek & jaw torn away, also teeth & part of tongue. He was most stoic as indeed are all the Black Watch as a whole.

A very awkward afternoon was Thursday. The French were making an offensive on our left & our artillery behind us had to shell continuously the Germans opposite. We were also to empty lead against their ramparts. The idea being our enemies would fear an attack & consequently bring up reserves, which might have gone elsewhere. Well we woke the Germans up & did much damage. They got some artillery up & shelled us back. It was quite lively for the time 1½ hours. Platoon commanders get a bad time on these occasions, as they usually do on all; they must go round the traverses of their platoons & cheer up their men, also seeing that all is correct. Luckily I have had a small place made in each traverse, of sandbags, this affords a little shelter from "blow-back" shells.

Some came very close, but their shooting mostly escaped my platoon of 42 men, though several smashed the parapet. By Friday I had only lost 1 man and that a corpl. Most luckily. Most people have suffered much worse, several being killed. There were many close shaves, however, of bullets cutting holes in glengarries, etc. German shells are beginning to deteriorate I think. Some contain pieces of glass, coke, & tiles or bricks. The rain & cold was most aggravating. Every night we worked hard at throwing earth up on to the rampart to repair & make more bullet proof. I chose the hours 12 to 4 A.M.

during the night. 2 A.M. is usually the quietest. All through the night the Germans sent up flares & rockets to light up the ground in front. We do not do this much, as the Germans are much more nervy and do it for us. It costs money. The effect of a flare is odd. Everyone ducks down & relief parties if coming try to appear nonexistent, but the Germans have most places sniped so that everywhere is dangerous. The flare shows up in ghastly relief ruined houses, one wall standing, beams swing in the eerie breeze, smashed up haystacks, & trees cut clear in half by shells. These trees present a very horrible sight. Something inexpressibly desolate & forlorn seems to be present and a deserted cat meowing in the distance would & should complete the scene, but it does not. In front, barely 100 yards away stands out in wild relief the German trenches, holed & broken, with barbed wire in front. Between the ramparts (they are not trenches, as these built months ago have become ditches filled to the brim with water, as the country is completely bogged) between the ramparts, I repeat, lay the unburied dead months old. Alas not Germans here, but the Highland Light Infantry who charged & were blown to pieces in German trench which was mined. Their dead are a piteous sight, flat on faces, arms stretched out, all facing the Germans as they fell. Here & there is one completely blown to pieces by a shell of our own which has fallen short. All are riddled with bullets from our own men as they lie on a fire-swept ground. First by night I thought them Germans & had an exceeding great joy, but in the morning on hearing & seeing the truth a great wave of horror assailed me, but tis nothing. Must relapse into notes again as time presses.

Friday was very cold, heavy rain. The Indians we consider here are of no use at all. Cannot explain now. All Friday occasional heavy fire & shelling. At 7.30 P.M. the Coldstreams relieved us. We lost 2 men, sniped, while leaving the approaches of the ramparts. Went to rest for the night about 400 yards back, where one stands a greater chance of petering out from shells than anywhere else. The Germans shell most houses once a day. All the houses are raked with bullets. I dug all night with a party up at the firing line ramparts. It's very dangerous & I fail to see how we are relieved, the work is more arduous and dangerous, because all snipers range on you. Shells very near billets all day, we moved a little further up towards trenches on Saturday [March 6] to Battalion headquarters. Five or six shells fell. Two unexploded picked up. It's all very interesting all this & I enjoy it. Took many photographs. At night digging in mud & water. Very cold night great frost with cold N. wind. Looks like a change in weather. Am afraid frostbite will be rampant.

The following is an unidentified letter typed by Lionel's family, dated 6 March 1915.

> We have now been up at the firing line for a week out of the 7 weeks (probable). Unfortunately there are no trenches (bog land), only ramparts of sandbags, with absolutely no cover behind from shells, result awfully dangerous. We got an awful shelling yesterday and the last few days, many casualties. I have had many wonderful escapes, indeed everyone has at least one or two a day, but to recount them anyone would think they were exaggerations. The shrapnel is rotten, a poor fellow next me [Corporal Gibb] got a couple of pellets right through the left jaw, part of his tongue out and all his gums and teeth. Awful wound. Several were killed. My platoon is fairly lucky so far, due to the sandbag holes I had made I think, but one has to walk round the traverses (6) to see the observers are on duty. That's the danger for me, as one has to go round every ten minutes to cheer them up. One merely laughs at the rifle fire. Their snipers are frightfully deadly. We have some <u>famous troops opposite</u>.* I should think it's highly possible I shall get wounded or something during 7 weeks of this inferno unless one has wonderful luck, unless you are here to see the shells, no one <u>can</u> understand it.

---

* Actually the 13th German Division directly opposite was considered weak. Lionel apparently refers here to the 11th Jäger Battalion in VII Corps Reserve.

8 The Battle of Neuve Chapelle

8 March–4 April 1915

The diary has been interrupted by a full week of frontline duty, but there survives a family copy of a letter written by Lionel to his mother on Monday, 8 March:

> Dear Mother,
>
> I snatch these few hours to write you a few lines, before we go back to the place which is as dangerous as this. Here I am sitting in a room only 500 yards from the trenches. We are supposed to be resting but that goes by the board. They shell us day and night, because we have some field pieces just behind. They circle round with shrapnel, high explosive, etc. so far they have missed us. Oh! it's simply fine. I don't know if my head is going or what, but I laugh and sometimes roar at the shells when they fly quite close. It takes people differently, others curse and swear at the Germans. Here I am—two shells fell 50 yards from the room where my servant shaved me this morning. I laughed and got cut on the lip by the razor. It's merely due to familiarity one has with them. I am exceptionally frightened of mice here, and had nasty dreams of one in a one hour sleep in a hole on the ground by our rampart. We are very angry we are not allowed our valises, even when out of the trenches for a few hours, which has always been allowed before, consequently we are done up and can get nothing, 6 months very long. It's for 6 months to come. I don't mind. Head and toes in mud I revel in everything. Its curious, isn't it? I have my walking stick in the trenches with only my revolver for attack. We are not allowed rifles. I snipe the Germans with a rifle from a wounded or dead man close by. Their snipers are wonderful shots. One poor fellow next me put up his head for a second to see where a shell from our gun had hit their parapet 100 yards off. Please excuse disconnected sentences, as really to write a letter is very difficult,

though to act in military matters is as clear as day to me the whole time, though of course whether one does the right thing or not is open to discussion. I was taught Bridge last night. We are frightfully cheerful the whole time. I have only got despondent twice, and that was at 12 midnight, curiously enough when nothing was doing and really I did feel sick of it, the outlook seemed so miserable, but as soon as work came on, it was different. We have been at it now since Feb. 28th, and had no rest and no sign. Poor fellow they got him through the jaw, gums, tongue, and came out tearing half his neck away. We bandaged him up somehow. Awful wound and in agony. The snipers have telescopic sights and special rifles, and so can shoot even the sights off our rifles at 100 and 150 yards. It's not wonderful really. We have few snipers with rifles as good. Their snipers are everywhere. The worst is we are enfiladed and can get shot at sideways, owing to the line being so smashed in. Where we are must remain a secret. I could not tell you, neither would I dream of saying who are next us who we relieved, except to say they were "blacks" and [we] laid them [bodies of dead Gurkhas] in their ramparts to stand on and fill up holes, also putting them the other side of the rampart to make it more bullet proof. Opposite we have a famous regiment and expect an attack every minute. Much damage was done. We have no head cover and no back cover, and what cover we have in front is not even bullet proof in places, all because we have no trenches as the land is bog and swamped. Not even dugouts to sleep, merely mud and bodies. No, the ramparts here are the only place no one will forget. They are rotten and get blown in every day. The German small shrapnel shells are becoming very inferior, they contain glass, bricks, cinders, and stones, sometimes even cinders, one burst against the breastworks in front of me, a sack was blown in and I proceeded to operate on it. I sliced it open and found in the earth a little portion of shell, some brick, etc. Most interesting. Cannot write clear now, there is no time.

However these events are chronicled in my brain, so as long as that organ remains and does not filter out. Some things are awful, but one becomes used to it. I have not seen such a thing like this before. The leading roads are studded with shell holes. Yesterday we were moving about and heard some Jack Johnsons and Black Marias, ploughing in a field. I am afraid they were sowing as well, because there were men about. One fell into a stream and a fountain flew up. There is no one in England or anywhere who can have the smallest molecule of an idea what its like out here, and when they casually read in the papers "Nothing of importance merely artillery duels," they forget the trenches are being shelled and people's lives are not only filtering out, but wounds and awful rain continue the same. We have suffered *from rain and having no dugouts, imagine 1 week of it, and also shelling. But remember one thing, we are all cheerful, fairly happy, and ready for anything, and do not complain, but one must have cheering news and plenty of it from home, and also say what is happening in the family, and if all is well. We think more of that than anything. All weekly papers (Scotch etc.) are much needed. The great thing is "Never contemplate or ponder." Keep filled up and then everyone would be as cheery as me, though the same thoughts affect one. There is only one thing I regret, and that is not being with the Argylls. The Black Watch is a nice regiment and is the premier one of Scotland, but to be "attached" takes a lot of spirit away.* I adored the Argylls ever so much, because the officers were some of the nicest people I have ever met, and so keen. Also the Col. Wilson quite one of the best and finest men in existence, and then Uncle Herbert was there. Here I have been landed in another regiment not knowing customs or a single man, except those I met at Havre. They are a great regiment and have not had any officers attached from other regiments before. I was the first to come and then. . . . there have been no others. I think they resented it, and consequently it was an uphill fight to get them accustomed. You can have no idea how a regiment such as this views the appearance of comparative strangers. Nevertheless despite our own vexation, we ploughed along, and I believe we are established at last. I have not shown to disadvantage in the firing line and I note there is a difference. One word—I believe an idea prevalent in England is that, the Subalterns or Second Lieutenants are foolish and get quickly cut up through foolishness. Remember a Platoon Commander has a great responsibility, acting on initiative etc. He has to encourage his men and expose himself more than anyone. For an attack he has to be in the front and first in everything. He is the first of all. No war has existed before like this, and they are bound to show promiscuously in the lists. Also there are more Second Lieutenants than usual with companies, quite 15 2nd Lieuts. against 20 Officers to a Battalion. Should much like a little chocolate, 2/- a week and 50 cigarettes every week, etc. Do not send things to the papers. I think much of you and all at home, but we are greatly occupied. etc.*

[Diary resumes] It is now Friday March 12th 1915, and at last we are getting a little rest of a few hours at the village of Le Touret 2 miles back from our

---

* Assigned temporarily to a unit other than one's own.

British Success Absolutely Complete

Great German Losses

The taking of Neuve Chapelle was a very brilliant piece of work. The attack was carefully prepared like everything else in the marvelous machine which the British Army has become and executed with a swiftness and a dash which ran the Germans off their feet. . . . Every soldier in Sir John French's Army today knows that, man for man, he is better than the German.

London Daily Mail, 15 March 1915

The capture of Neuve Chapelle last week is the most striking success won by our armies since the Battle of Ypres. After subjecting the Germans to a terrific bombardment we advanced for three quarters of a mile over a front of 4,000 yards. So heavily had the Germans suffered from our shell-fire that they were unable to offer any effective resistance. Their elaborate series of trenches were filled with dead and dying, and it is estimated that their losses amounted to 17,000 including 1720 prisoners.

London Graphic, 20 March 1915

rampart lines. As the offensive is still on, we may have to advance any minute, but I forgot I have not mentioned the advance yet.

Well, we have been in the ramparts nearly 2 weeks with ceaseless toil, since even if you were the Company in Reserve, you had a worse time than in the ramparts. All day the company works on piling sandbags up against the one house which has not suffered much from shellfire. This is Battalion headquarters. All day we get shelled at intervals and indeed the escapes one has are enormous. There is an observation post at the top of a haystack 20 yards away. Consequently they draw fire on to us. At night one has to go up to the firing line & repair damage to trenches, also improving the support line trenches 100 to 200 yards in rear. One is sniped at the whole time and occasionally a "minenwerfer" gets on to you. We work as a rule with sappers & the R.E.s [Royal Engineers]. They had four dead one night & 7 wounded. There is no head cover until you build one up with sandbags. One has also to approach the places by Chocolat Menier Corner & Princes Street, ludicrous names, as it should be called Snipers' Street, Bomb House, Dead Cow House being the way the extreme left company of the battalion working in this section, would use.

Well, on Tuesday night [9 March] the great event came. . . . General Haig, commanding the 1st Army Corps,* i.e. that army whose main front is the Armentières–La Bassée region, issued a pamphlet, each platoon commander getting one, on which was written a few words. But such words. Surely no words ever had greater meaning, & will ever be again the forerunner of such joy which should soon fill all British citizens.

Special Order.
To the 1st Army.

We are about to engage the enemy under very favourable conditions. Until now in the present campaign, the British Army has, by its pluck and determination, gained victories against an enemy greatly superior both in men and guns. Reinforcements have made us stronger than the enemy on our front. Our guns are now both more numerous than the enemy's are, and also larger than any hitherto used by any army in the field. Our Flying Corps has driven the Germans from the air.

On the Eastern Front, and to South of us, our Allies have made marked progress and caused enormous losses to the Germans, who are, moreover, harassed by internal troubles and shortage of supplies, so that there is little prospect at present of big reinforcements being sent against us here.

In front of us we have only one German Corps, spread out on a front as large as that occupied by the whole of our Army (the First).

We are now about to attack with about 48 battalions a locality on that front which is held by some three German battalions. It seems probable, also that for the first day of the operations the Germans will not have more than four battalions of reinforcements for the counter attack. Quickness of movement is therefore of first importance to enable us to forestall the enemy and thereby gain success without severe loss. At no time in this war has there been a more favourable moment for us, and I feel confident of success. The extent of that success must depend on the rapidity and determination with which we advance.

Although fighting in France, let us remember that we are fighting to preserve the British Empire and to protect our homes against the organized savagery of the German Army. To ensure success, each of us must play his part, and fight like men for the Honour of Old England.

D. HAIG, General
Commanding 1st Army.
9th March, 1915.

---

* Haig was in command of the First Army, not I Corps (as of 26 December 1914).

It was the advance, the much discussed & ever longing event expected by a great nation. The men received the news very stolidly, as befit men who know what war is like, & the cost an advance entails. However it needed no uninitiated person to explain their feelings, their appearance was of men ready to go through anything for their Empire & regiment, but of men who desire rest after much shaking up of nerves and system.

The communication although confident of our superiority in numbers, was without doubt too keen to underrate.

That night there were great preparations. There was also great rain & cold wind. I was up all night digging as we had just become company in Reserve. They shelled us that night & killed several men on the road with high explosives & shrapnel shells. At 3.30 A.M. I got back. Really the escapes one has from stray bullets is extraordinary & verily my luck is in. Two fellows got holes in their cap comforters. At 5.30 A.M. I was up feeling very tired as really, my average rest has been 2 hours per night, usually less, and certainly no sleep. There was some mistake about breakfast, as Captain Kedie* having arrived the previous night with Second Lieut. Purvis & 45 men, Edwards had to go back to D Company & take command. The order is this now:

> B Company: Captain Kedie
> No. 5 Platoon 2/Lt. L. F. Sotheby
> No. 6 Platoon 2/Lt. Purvis
> No. 7 Platoon 2/Lt. Merrilees
> No. 8 Platoon 2/Lt. L. Hay
> Company Sergeant Major Winchester

Well, breakfasts were late and they had to be over by 6.50 A.M. as the bombardment previous to advance was to start at 7.30 A.M. Breakfast finally came & while we were arranging, the bombardment started. The noise was colossal, hundreds of guns must have been firing as our guns had been coming up daily. The bombardment, all say, is the heaviest so far experienced during this war. I say this because it is not yet over. It started 7.30 A.M. & continued till 11 A.M. so fiercely that to speak was almost impossible when the intention was to be heard. From 11 A.M. till 1 P.M. today (another 26 hours) the shelling was very severe, every now & then rivalling its earlier vigour. But guns cannot fire forever & they gradually eased off. 5 Field pieces just behind us kept on firing volleys & the noise was great. But I will go into the smaller details later. From

---

* Captain W. T. Kedie, later killed at the Dardanelles.

1 P.M. till now, about 7 P.M. the bombardment had occasional bursts. Really the noise was awful & some of the men got nasty headaches. The damage to the Germans must have been terrible. Indeed here is one instance. All our trenches are connected by telephone to the artillery & the different headquarters. During the first morning of the inferno, one of our forward redoubts by means of glasses distinguished a great mass of Germans collecting behind some hay stacks & hedge. About 600 of them. Accordingly the telephone was used to our heavy artillery. Within 1 minute 8 enormous high explosive shells called "Mothers" or "Wifes," a smaller type or practically the same as Jack Johnsons & Black Marias, exploded in the exact spot & the entire spot was obliterated. Objects were said to fly about & these were thought to be legs & arms & other parts of the body mingled with earth. Our artillery has greatly improved.

During the whole time the Germans replied very scantily, indeed it seemed as if they had run short of guns, though on the next day, we got it here rather badly, as during the night they had rushed up some heavy guns. Consequently the "coalboxes," a nickname given to a very powerful shell slightly smaller than the grave diggers or Black Marias. These at 9 A.M. and 12 noon were quite numerous & our two outbuildings on the left hand side of the road to the left of headquarters received several. Great damage was done. The holes they plough are roughly 7 feet or 10 feet wide & four feet or 5 feet deep. In a house the damage done is far greater and the effect of dust & smoke truly enough to awe one. Many whistled just above us, & exploded further on, indeed one caught a big tree sideways taking out a great mouthful. Shrapnel followed each time. Luckily only 5 men got shrapnel wounds outside in the road. Quite close. The Reserve company of the Camerons was having a rifle inspection by platoons. One shrapnel burst on one section & wounded 13 men, some very badly indeed. Our casualties were very light in comparison to those suffered by the enemy.

At 4 P.M. on Wednesday, the first day [10 March] the Second Black Watch, 7th Division (Meerut), Indian Expeditionary Force was reported to have captured 300 Germans, mostly dressed in old clothes, some in civilian garb.

The bombardment was naturally to demoralize & smash up the enemy's ramparts. The line of the Great Offensive is from Neuve Chapelle to Givenchy, 1 mile west of La Bassée. Both at Givenchy & Neuve Chapelle great forward motions were to be carried out, the centre, _i.e._ that region of Festubert & the few miles to the north, with mainly the 1st Brigade, 1st Division, was to draw the enemy's fire & to make them believe we were attacking, if signs of a German evacuation of those ramparts to our immediate front became evident, we were to charge forward, otherwise wait for the advance to be given us by signal. We had to pour in colossal rifle fire all the first morning & then slacken off. We believe the attacks were most successful as by 11 A.M. the British had advanced 2 miles, & by nighttime the report was La Bassée had fallen, but I am somewhat skeptical thereof.

There was sadness in the morning. Haldane had been wounded in the leg, & the new officer who came the other [day] & wears spectacles, got badly wounded in the head. We had several casualties among the men. Several men were killed & wounded on the road between here & the ramparts about 500 yards off at one point.

I was up digging on Wednesday night till 5 A.M. During the night the Germans made a small counterattack which was repulsed. My men were in the open just behind our ramparts, and as the shells & bullets were unhealthy we got together & stood to arms. After 20 or 30 minutes, things were fairly quiet, so we continued. 1 German coalbox landed very close in a ditch by Princes Street & made an awful mess. We only had 12 shovels, so we arranged for reliefs of my platoon to come up every 1 hour & 20 minutes. A little description of the first few hours' firing is necessary as we had to hurry out of our 3 smashed up houses & sit down in the small ramparts erected immediately behind the buildings & facing our own guns who by the way nearly blew us up once or twice as there were a few bad time fuses.

Well here is a very bad description of a bombardment which is the forerunner of a great advance. At 7.30 A.M. an earsplitting and thundering noise of hundreds of guns on our side suddenly lent their music of subtle influence to the gently moving breeze. For one second everyone felt slightly dazed, then being on the spot I got my men to our ramparts slightly to the rear of our billets or ruins opposite to headquarters. No. 6 platoon was behind the other ruins & the other 2 platoons were behind a hospital 100 yards lower down. Situated in this position I was able to consider the situation. The enemy were so surprised & stupefied that for ½ an hour they did [not] fire a shot in answer & all we got were a few headaches. Indeed several old campaigners got severe ones. After the first half hour the enemy started to answer back with a very slight fire compared with our own. Several "coalboxes," the lesser Jack Johnsons, landed behind us & smashed part of our billet ruins still more. Several real Jack Johnsons burst to the left of us doing little damage. The enemy then let loose with high explosive shrapnel, many of which struck our ruins showering mud & dust over us. The left hand corner of our ruin was carried right away. Luckily nobody was there. Several shrapnel bullets & pieces of shell landed in the rampart, but no one was hurt. These pieces I have in my possession including a piece of brass ring from a "coalbox."

The German shells were however of little consequence. Ours however had enormous effect & the German ground must have been totally smashed up. The noise of shells was wonderful. Howitzers and field guns of every description mingled themselves with the French 75s which loosed off in great volleys.* Then would come the sullen roar of our 5 inch naval guns & some of even greater calibre. Some of our shrapnel fell short, but not much harm was done. The noise was most curious as a peculiar whirring noise was set up in the trees. One could hear the shells whistling by indeed it seemed odd not to be able to see them so distant was the noise as they flew by overhead.

Thursday night [11 March] we came down from the ramparts to the little village of Le Touret 1¾ miles back. We left under one of the heaviest rifle fires that many of our people have so far experienced. A heavy bombardment was also on, and our route pitted on all sides by "coalboxes," etc.

The Coldstreams relieved us. We marched into Le Touret very tired & there at 12 midnight I saw my valise after 2 weeks non change. Unluckily we were under orders to proceed at 10 minutes' notice to the line again, and so we were unable to get a change. Indeed I was so tired that I just flopped down & slept like a log till 5.30 A.M. Have had no rest for 2 weeks, as the only time our company was reserve for 2 nights I was up all night digging at the ramparts. My shirt is 3 weeks old as I had it on at Burbure as well. Equipment has also been on 2 weeks & one at last does not notice it.

Well all Friday [12 March] we stood to arms in a field, ready to go up any minute. The Germans had got up some heavy guns in the night & started to smash up Le Touret where we are. The shells were of the Black Maria type, & did awful damage. D Company's field kitchen got damage. A huge shell burst 20 yards off smashing up the kitchen, killed a Coldstream, also 3 horses, wounding others & then killed the cook who was cut to pieces. Awful damage was done [to] parts of the village which curiously enough had not been shelled before. An old woman was cut in half by a shell before it burst. Several peasants were also killed. Our headquarters also got a few. Our guns soon silenced the Germans because the shelling only lasted 2 hours. It was a cold day and messages concerning our progress by Neuve Chapelle were very frequent. Statements official said that Germans were surrendering in large numbers.

---

* The Seventy-fives (75 mm.) were highly mobile, quick-firing French field guns.

Severe bayonet fights had been fought. Later on, that is to say this morning, Saturday [13 March] we were told that the attacks from Givenchy directed against La Bassée had failed. The Germans threw petrol bombs at the wounded & then shot them down when trying to rise. On the left close to us the 2nd Black Watch lost 8 officers 150 men killed & wounded. One batch of prisoners taken were all slaughtered because one of their number suddenly shot down an officer. The Gurkhas fought very well using their kukris [swords] with great success. We have advanced 4 miles on our left. Our guns are said to have quite demoralized the Germans, who are suffering from shattered nerves. The bombardment is said to have been the heaviest of the war so far. Thousands and thousands of shells being fired. We the first Brigade were in the very centre of this inferno and even war-worn veterans declare it gave them awful headaches. Luckily the Germans did not reply in anything like the same way. Prisoners state that the Germans have 30,000 reserves in Lille, & these are being rushed up against us as well as guns. We have been shelled at intervals during the day but the Black Watch have had no casualties. Our troops are pouring in. We are off to the trenches tonight to relieve the Coldstream Guards, so we shall catch it alright. Shall have no time to write again probably for sometime.

~

MARCH 15 (MONDAY) Second day in the ramparts again and most interesting. Haldane it should be said was not wounded as previously stated. We only lost 1 officer during the great bombardment but the second Black Watch on our left lost 8 officers and 30 men killed and wounded.

News has also come in that the "Seaforths" did very very well. They waited until the Germans got quite close in their usual mass and then volleyed at them. Only 1 German reached the ramparts, all the rest were mown down. It is said that the Seaforths behaved just as on peace parades in Scotland & their discipline was excellent.

There is a stupid idea prevalent at the base in England that Regiments at the front must be so cut up as to make cohesion in all duties an impossibility. Also that the regiments are one continual stream of drafts, & therefore the 1st Division is bound to be recalled. However when once you reach the front all this altered. You notice at a glance that the battalions, or at least this battalion, are well together & not messed up anyhow. How is this? Well a continual stream is always arriving of the original regulars who have been previous[ly] wounded. These well together & consolidate the others. But this not all. Every 5 or 6 weeks a regiment or a brigade or Division will be relieved at the trenches and rest for 2 weeks or so. They then get thoroughly together, & some lucky ones get leave. No. I think the regiments (Regulars) are as good as ever. The 1st Division will not be withdrawn because practically everyone in it has by now seen service, so that to shift it right away would be of no advantage. The men get their few weeks' rest every month or so, though during that period much practice work is done. Kitchener's army will not be placed in a lump. That notion is absurd. For these trying circumstances & conditions of heavy artillery, brand new Battalions might get a sort of stage fright, so that the presence of the war-worn soldier is needed not only as a stimulant, but to remind newcomers that they have thoroughly seasoned troops on either side.

I am writing now in one of the small redoubts called "Grouse Butts." There is no shelter of any description, merely a rough semi-circular heap of sand bags with a few 6 feet behind & only 2 feet high as back cover. The sand bags are in some places not even bullet proof, so the conditions are somewhat trying. This part of the line is most loosely held. My platoon of 40 men and 2 telephone orderlies are holding 5 of these butts, our line extending 400 yards. On our left again is another Battalion which also has 5 "grouse butts" for its left flank. Thus 10 butts each having 1 NCO & 6 men have to defend about 800 to 1000 yards. Our rear line (defensive) is strong but this is about the weakest part of the line. There is absolutely no cover between the butts. Not even a communication trench as the old trenches are still full to the brim with water & partly fallen in. There is also no cover for approaching the butts from the rear. "Dead Cow Farm" is our support & reserve base for B Co'y.

Thus no one can move or stir out of the butts by day, as they would get shot at once. 3 men were wounded the other day, & the Coldstreams had 5 killed in 3 days at this one spot.

I write all this under difficulties as I am sitting in this weird butt & a fairly heavy shelling is going on but completely missing us as it is the [rival] artillery looking for each other, or one or the other shelling the roads most used by transport troops. We had a trench mortar on us at 2 P.M. but no damage was done to flesh luckily. They shelled "Dead Cow Farm" at 1 P.M. I hope the remainder of the Company remained unscathed, for it was pretty heavy.

It is now 4.30 P.M. Today has been very warm and very like spring. But the sun did not come out, so I had to take "time exposures." The larks are curiously enough singing merrily although the shells must whiz by them now and then. Recently there has not been a bird to be seen. Close to the rear of this butt there is a huge tree practically severed 20 feet from the ground by a shell. Its upper part has fallen towards us & several sparrows are busily engaged in nesting already. A curious contrast indeed. Peace with the birds but war with the more intellectual & civilized parts of life, namely man.

~

MARCH 16 (TUESDAY) The last biscuits reached me the other night in some isolated "Butts" only approachable by night, as there are no communication ramparts and you approach over open ground swept by the enemy's fire. Luckily at night they cannot see you except when the flares go up. Then you lie flat down, or perhaps lose a man, but it has to be done, these are the advance posts in one district. They have no lavatories and you can only get three yards to the back as you then get enfilades. We are three days at a time here, and no fires are allowed or smoking by night. I am sitting in my butt now with 1 NCO, 86 men and 2 telephone operators, the only connection with other life. We were shelled this morning but no casualties. An hour ago I had the "pleasure" of seeing "Dead Cow Farm" our support house, shelled also. I am here for 3 days, it's the worst place so far. I had the narrowest shave of my life the first night. Everyone has constantly narrow shaves from stray bullets or snipes, but my luck this time was genuine. In front of the "butts" are a few posts and a little barbed wire put down three or four months ago when the Germans were driven back from the ground we now hold. My company commander said that if possible wire should be put down in front. Accordingly determining to see the work done properly I took a man called Watson and one reel of barbed wire and sallied out from my "Grouse butt" at 3.30 A.M. We reached the posts 20 to 30 yards from the "redoubts" or "butts" between the Germans and the British. Flares flew up every minute or so outlining us plainly. There is not a bit of cover between us and the Germans. It is grass as flat as a billiard table, as the line is a "salient" here they shoot flares from behind, outlining and silhouetting you horribly. For five minutes we worked, falling flat every now and then, unsniped at. Then for fifteen minutes we got sniped at occasionally. At the end of 25 minutes the snipers had warned everyone and we had five or six volleys fired at us, no effect. We relocated. After three or four minutes we continued and were just finishing the reel, having done 30 yards or so of front of fairly good entanglement, when they sent up three or four of the brightest rockets I have seen yet. It was as light as day and every post stood out plainly, even the wire. A perfect fusillade greeted us, and my companion whom I had had to constantly swear at to get him to unreel the wire, suddenly fell sideways on the ground practically touching me. He was shot through the leg (knee)—I stayed there for three minutes and had the worst time of my life, expecting a bullet to find me every minute. The flares then subsided and I dashed over the intervening 30 yards and fell exhausted for a second into a "grouse butt." I then got a volunteer to come out at once and we fetched him in, having great trouble with the flares. We bandaged him up and had him conveyed away. I now hear that through the gross carelessness of a N.C.O. or someone the message was not sent along the line telling that we were going out barbed-wiring. Consequently the extreme right "butt" seeing two figures creeping about also fired at us, and only recognized us when the flare of light was at its fiercest. The N.C.O. or whoever was responsible for the message not getting through will get it pretty hot when we leave these butts. Frankly I do not want to repeat the nasty job. The only way to barb wire, is for the engineers to bring up spiked lengths of wire which you place down every 6 yards and then dash in for another section. But we cannot get it. Just at present I am feeling sublimely happy, and content with things, but every now and then I long to return to England and for a "slight" rest. Beyond a chest cough I am all right, the other is cured. It does not matter what you get, no one retires from the line unless absolutely done in, or wounded or. . . . One can't afford it, as everyone has some small complaint. Once you leave the firing line with some illness, it is like being wounded, you return to England and take your turn in coming out. I have no intention of leaving the line, it amuses me intensely, as one becomes totally callous of the dead and death that are around you. Horrible to say this is the truth.

I don't know what I shall be like after this war, I feel I am passing through a peculiar stage, just as a caterpillar becomes a chrysalis and then a butterfly. I cannot explain. It comes unseen and makes you oblivious of almost everything at times, save one intense desire to kill, kill, kill, the Germans in front. I loosed off 200 rounds of ammunition yesterday at a party of relief (Germans). It was impossible to see the result as darkness was rapidly approaching. But 50 shots went there anyhow. I think "reliefers" come up that way, accordingly I poured in shots from 5 P.M. to 8 P.M. the most likely times. Sometimes I get bored as it seems one has to remain out until you get wounded or killed, at other times I live in a perfect heaven fairly revelling in and enjoying the ramparts immensely.

~

MARCH 24 (WEDNESDAY) I have got a beastly cold again now, as we had deep snow the other day, and it was awful in the ramparts, as there was absolutely no protection and a regular blizzard raged on and off for three days.

I had to return my camera as they are forbidden in all regiments both home and abroad, 6 others have had to do so in the regiment. I am enjoying myself immensely out here, but would much like a few days' leave.

It is now Saturday, March 27th. Some time has elapsed since I last entered anything in my diary. It has been impossible, however, our time has been much occupied. Much fighting occurred about the 20th when a blizzard of snow came in the night & made things awful and we had no shelters. During the 21st, however, the sun shone in a perfect azure sky & the heat was most appreciated. In the night it snowed again. Much artillery fighting was a great feature. The Coldstreams were using a trench mortar on the 22nd, when a shell came and of the two men left a cannibal could scarcely have got a mouthful. Much parapet on the right was blown in, as also was much of the Germans'. On the 21st the Germans opposite who are believed to be Bavarians started singing and calling us names. Our men not slow to reply shouted epithets back, one epithet in particular being the Tommies' favorite home & abroad. Our men have got into the way of calling the Germans "Allemands" but pronouncing it not in the French way, but after the fashion of an uneducated person. Thus the "e" is pronounced long. A favourite epithet is "allemands how you was."

We came out of the trenches on Wednesday 24th for 5 days' rest. Our destination was Hinges about 3 miles in a direct line from the firing line. It was raining heavily when we left the ramparts, and was fairly dark. Although Hinges is only 3 miles away the route there is by no means straight. Wednesday night in particular made it seem still worse. We left Le Touret at 6.30 P.M. and arrived Hinges 10 P.M.! Three and three quarter hours. A good bit of the delay is due to the bad roads, twisting & turning about. They seem to follow all the ditches. This is by no means an exaggeration. In countless places the road actually twisted back not as a snake, but angularly, straight in between. It did not shorten the journey by taking the wrong road once or twice or by getting hopelessly lost once.

At length we arrived Hinges. The second night Thursday I took off my kilt, the first time for 30 days, I certainly did not expect to find what I did: namely, thousands & thousands of eggs inside the creases in various parts thereof. Also worse still the crawly ones were there, hundreds of them, & seemingly of the Gurkha species a slightly larger variety with a forked and poisonous tongue, so it is said. It was a sad discovery & one I am every minute deploring. The eggs we kill in the thousands, but they still hatch out. Another few days, & had we not found them out, I should have been a walking mass probably not being able to go where I wanted to, different parts of my body wanting to go different ways. Luckily this has not yet come to pass. I believe sitting in front of a warm fire hatched the first installment out and as serials were certain to follow, of course the hot iron was the best thing together with Keating's beetle powder. I am afraid my servant Jamieson was so zealous to eliminate this distressing plague that he burnt pieces out of the kilt. Were it not with the certain belief that a bug or two had got with it, I might also feel slightly bored.

By now Saturday 27th we have the bugs well under. Last night the sole bag was only 30, when heating up all possible "coverts" in the kilt. However one rather unnerving discovery was feeling a crawly one on my neck. Giving my hand a quick cant on to the back of the head, I found I had dislodged two of the Gurkha variety who had been attempting either to dig themselves when crossing open country or were merely airing themselves. On a quick examination of my shirt, 20 or so were found. I still have hopes of getting them under by Monday when I believe we return to the ramparts. Not much of a rest this time, indeed it hardly is a rest. The fighting at St. Eloi & Neuve Chapelle has ceased.

Strong Position of the Allies

The Week's Fighting Reviewed

It is just a week since the battle of the north has resumed and flamed out with greater intensity than ever along the whole line from Arras to the sea.

Now the events of the week stand out in their true perspective, and it is possible to form some estimate of the general position. As the official *communiqués* put it, the situation remains good for us; so good, indeed, that the armies of the Allies are inspired with increasing confidence and cheerfulness. A glance at the position along the line will show that confidence and cheerfulness are amply justified.

The Attack on Aubers Ridge

Below Armentières our line runs through the Bois Grenier, Givenchy, and Cuinchy, on the western outskirts of La Bassée. This has been the black spot of the week. Here it was that we stormed the slopes of the Aubers Ridge, stormed them unsuccessfully and at heavy cost because we had not sufficient high explosives at our command to destroy the strong German entrenchments on the hilltops.

But our men who fell on the Aubers slopes did not fall altogether in vain. The menace of the Aubers Ridge deceived the enemy. He withdrew his troops from regions further south to defend his salient at La Bassée. Though the attack failed we menace La Bassée still and hold in our front a large force of the enemy. Thus we are rendering service to the French in the Lens-Arras sector. And so from the sea to La Bassée the fair land of Belgium and French Flanders is belted by the united armies of Belgium, France and Britain. At no point has the enemy a favourable prospect of breaking through.

Times, 17 May 1915

9   Aubers Ridge

7–24 May 1915

My dear Nigel,

    The Battle for Aubers Ridge, Richebourg, in which we took part on May 9th Sunday has had much readable matter given to it in the papers. Much of this is grossly inaccurate.

    On Saturday evening we were withdrawn from the front line & support ramparts & herded together in the reserve ramparts, our place being filled by the 2nd & 3rd Brigades. The Northamptons & Sussex relieved us putting 2 battalions where we originally had 1 only. It was a cold night though starlight & it was a curious sight seeing these other regiments file along to their allotted ramparts passing Chocolat Menier Corner & then crossing the Rue du Bois. They had all left their packs in Béthune because of the morrow's charge. They all seemed quite lively. Two Northampton officers were hit by bullets while coming up. At last all the men had gone to other positions & quiet reigned except for occasional shots. Apparently some Germans shouted across to the Sussex "English how you do? Where is your offensive, Englishmen?" etc. They had obviously learnt of our preparations & were ready.

    1.30 A.M. all quiet. 3 A.M. daylight started. 3.30 A.M. artillery officers strolled carelessly along to various ruined houses, where their observation stations were. They assembled in little groups smoking & chatting, just as the first rays of the sun shone upon them. Perfect stillness, a lark singing & smoke gently rising from their cigarettes, it was difficult to believe that through the instrumentality of these few in two hours' time lives would be as cheap as ants' eggs. To these men was given the power of hurling shells, the only way to attack the enemy. 4 A.M. one by one they sauntered into their stations. 4.15 A.M. a dull scream overhead followed by a deep roar ½ a mile away told us that "Mother" or "Grannie" had started on the enemy's stronghold redoubts. "Mother" & a few "Wives" (5.7's) (9 inches) etc. were fired intermittently till 5 A.M. At 5 A.M. a terrific cannonade broke the erstwhile calm. Such a bom-

bardment as is rarely heard. However the guns seemed to be directing their fire chiefly to the left of us, only a few falling on our sector. We (the different divisions) were attacking on a 2½ mile front. During the whole bombardment our heavy guns seemed to devote their attention to the left. 5.15 P.M. Enemy started shelling us with pip squeaks & high explosive shrapnel, an awful deadly weapon. Each ball of which when the shell bursts 30 feet up, will make a hole in the ground big enough to place a cricket ball in. Its radius of death is about 100 by 50 yards or more according to height of burst. 5.30 P.M. Above the tumult we could hear heavy rifle fire & bullets whizzed over in thousands. Our infantry were charging. It was then we were told to move.

We rushed along behind a network of breastworks & eventually came to the spot where we had to leap over & cross the open Rue du Bois & then open fields to the Support Rampart.

The enemy were now shelling vigourously with shrapnel & the bullets tore up the ground everywhere. Casualties now appeared. The ambulance men of different regiments were rushing about, dashing over ramparts picking up casualties. Streams of wounded, slightly wounded & others were tearing about, arms roughly bandaged & legs & heads similarly swathed. The excitement was intense. How far have we advanced yelled some of our men. "Taken enemy's third line trenches," yelled back these warriors who had never even reached <u>our</u> first line, but had been wounded by shrapnel when rushing up from the support to the firing line ramparts a distance of about 500 yards. Nevertheless they all thought it was their business to bring some news. (You see they were doing their little bit.) This stream of wounded dashing about caused much wonderment from new arrivals. Occasionally dead men were strewn about. I tried to get the rifle from one man but he held it too fast even in death.

At last, how we did it I don't know, we reached the support ramparts. Occasionally I looked over and saw something which showed me at once we were in for it. High explosive shrapnel & common shrapnel was sweeping the 500 yards of communication rampart leading up to the front line. A solid wall of shells seemed to be everywhere. The enemy's ramparts & all the country for further than 800 yards was in a fog of yellow smoke, through which flashes appeared. These fumes literally darkened the sun. All around were crashing branches & trees being felled. Occasionally a huge shell would land in a ruined house & the brick dust would form a London fog in itself. There was barely a breath of air, so the fog & smoke hung everywhere. Above was a deep blue azure sky with a bright sun, both becoming dim through the smoke. Above again were our airplanes, puffs of white smoke bursting around them.

Every now & then a huge black smoke shell would blow up in our rampart killing & maiming people. Campbell, Merrilees's servant, was unrecognizable minus two arms, head & 1 leg. Carson in my platoon was worse off as his remains could have been buried in a cigarette case. Meanwhile heavy German rifle fire was sweeping overhead so I kept under the parapet. It seemed impossible to me that we could ever reach the first line, and for 1 minute I felt a little rotten, the only time during the day. The whole point is once you are on the move you have not got time to think of dangers. At last 6 A.M. we march off. I was the last platoon. We rushed along the communication [trench] at awful speed. The wounded were crawling about in the passage & dead there were innumerable. At last only losing 3 men we reached the front line. But what a sight. It was 6 deep & in places 7 deep with men. All regiments, KRRs [King's Royal Rifles], Northamptons, Sussex, Scots Guards, Loyal Lancs, etc. I rushed my men to the left where I saw some Black Watch people & hastily made the line a little thicker. I enquired the cause of so many men being assembled there while such a hellish fire from the Germans was blotting them out now & then. They said the attack had failed. The German parapet was little damaged & the wire more or less intact. The Northamptons & Lancs had been mown down, few getting anywhere near the enemy's parapet, here 400 yards away, flat ground.

Rum jars innumerable lay about, which showed that those who charged at 5.30 A.M. had been given something for their spirits. Gradually wounded and lightly wounded Northamptonshires crawled to the parapet one by one & some of our gallant fellows hauled them in. We rescued some 50 men. One fellow got an awful shock as he found he was hauling in a "bomb man" who fairly bristled with these things round his waist. The Germans sniped at the wounded & our men who tried to help them. Some wounded were awful sights, broken legs & arms & covered with mud, blood flowing in streams. One or two unwounded crawled in, including a wounded officer who had lost all his nerves & was talking nonsense. The dead & dying in the ramparts was beastly. Numbers could have been buried in sandbags, or even biscuit boxes.

Wonderful wasn't it. We were supposed to have advanced to 3 trenches away & here we were a few thousand casualties & only the hope of similar casualties on the German side from our own fire. At 12 noon we were told we would assault again at 2 P.M. This was cancelled. At 3 P.M. we were told to return to the Reserve ramparts. We got halfway & were suddenly told to return. On getting back to the firing line the order came. Bombardment 3.20 P.M. attack 3.55 P.M. Now we were for it. Packs were ordered to be taken off &

piled. Our sensations were odd. It had been one day of disappointment &
muddle in a sense, but every man was ready for a similar fate as befell the
others in the morning. The bombardment started & the Germans replied with
one almost as heavy. They had brought more guns up in the afternoon. Heavy
"coal-boxes," 5 inch & 9 inch, flew about, & our casualties were severe. Our
C.O. was marvelous.

3.55 P.M. We charged. You know the result—15 officers killed & wounded,
I the only survivor. 500 men killed & wounded. Barbed wire practically intact.
I managed to return at 8.15 P.M. The Camerons on the left only attacked with
only 1 company because the order for attack came before they were ready.
More muddle. Thus 1 Battalion & 1 company attacked where 2 Brigades failed
in the morning & in places (2) some men found a gap to crawl to the parapet,
indeed in one place 2 traverses were actually held for a few minutes. I was on
the extreme right of the attack, & returned after with 4 men!

[unsigned]

~

May 11, 1915

My dear Mother,

Perhaps you have heard about it by now. The awful losses on Sunday
which was to have been the great advance. The old fault, wire not cut.

The Black Watch including myself charged the German trenches 400
yards away. The whole 15 officers were killed, except 4. Of these 4, 3 were
wounded & I survived. I tell you it was a miracle and I feel quite changed as
I lay out 15 yards from the German trenches for 4 hours before crawling back.

The attack in the morning failed. Our shelling was bad as it failed to cut
the wire, though thousands of German dead lay behind the trenches so the
aeroplanes report. We were rushed up to the front trenches through a hellish
fire of shrapnel and heavy gun fire. Many were killed and wounded. The
enemy had got wind of the attack, got up huge reinforcements and guns. The
high explosive shrapnel shells were fearful, sweeping the ground for yards. All
the communication ramparts were swept continually. However we reached
the first line ramparts to discover the attack had failed. I think the failure of
cutting the wire was due to bombarding too wide a front and not doing it
thoroughly. Well, the Germans shelled us very hard in the ramparts then, and
many were killed. The day was cloudless, but the smoke from bursting shells
made quite a fog over everything. Wounded men crept over the parapet and
were hauled in.

This went on all day until 12 noon, when we were told we would attack again. We charged at 4 P.M. I in charge of No. 5 and Wallace* in charge of No. 6 in B Co'y charged with the Battalion. That is 15 officers. The German trenches were 350 to 400 yards away, and had been bombarded again before the attack. We ran 50 yards and then perforce had to walk the remainder. Many of the men actually stopping and firing at the Germans [who were] look[ing] over and firing from their parapets. In places the machine guns wiped men out very rapidly (3 officers were wounded, 11 killed, and myself unhurt). I was on the extreme right with my platoon and we had no one attacking on our left, thus we got cross-fire.

By the time I reached the German wire, I had only 4 or 5 men left with me and we found the wire <u>uncut</u>!

150–200 yards on our left there was a gap and A Company was getting through all massed together, they were mown down, quite a number however getting into the German rampart. Being only 15 yards from the Germans who were fighting [firing] over their parapet at us, it was impossible to get to that gap, so we sought cover. There were a few shell holes close to the wire and into them we got, firing at the Germans above. We did some good as it prevented them getting a cross-fire into our men getting over on the left a good distance away. We accounted for several. One big German in a helmet stood waist high above the parapet firing and raving at us. I think we got him.

A signaller of ours was right under the lee of the German parapet and bravely kept signalling back various messages, he was 200 yards to the left. As a result our artillery observers directed gun fire on the left and right flanks, and where some of our men got through the wire, in order to protect them a bit, as a result we got a bit of the shelling being a long way to the right. My cap fell off before I got into the small shell hole and was lying 3 yards away outside. We all wore our caps with the Balaclava helmets on top. My cap has about 7 holes from shrapnel and pieces of shell! Lucky it wasn't my head! An explosion from one of the shells stunned me for about 10 minutes. The Germans were well down now and were sniping from loop holes near the base of the parapet. They sniped at anything that moved, wounded and all. Thus we few that were left dug ourselves as low as possible. I was wedged in between 2 dead men. Lce. Cpl. Swan† on my left and someone else on my right. Swan

---

* 2/Lt. J. Wallace, commissioned from the ranks (March 1915) after nineteen years and nine months' service, was one of the officers killed on this day.

† Lce. Cpl. D. Swan, bomb thrower.

was shot through the forehead. These two dead men protected me somewhat from shrapnel of our own guns.

In the charge and while in the hole at first, I had two shots through my haversack and one through the strap of my equipment ½ inch off the flesh. Another shot hit my entrenching tool and smashed it in half. The metal end hit me in the back very hard, making me think I was wounded at first in the back. Never shall I forget that awful experience. For 4 hours (4 P.M. to 8 P.M.) I lay there cramped up and never moved once. I am still stiff and very sore on the right side of the head where a lump of dry earth gave me an awful bang, when a shell burst.

I was afraid a shell would land on me, as our artillery bombarded the Germans continuously over us and we only 15 yards from them. It was awful. I was also afraid they would chuck bombs at us lying there, they did later at the wounded, petrol bombs. But I had crawled back by then. I waited there till 8 P.M. and then being a bit dark I attempted to crawl back. It was rotten and how the snipers missed me is wonderful. The ground was perfectly flat the whole 400 yards. It took me 30 minutes to crawl back, and then on getting over our parapet, I had to rest a bit. Finding the Battalion had left to go to Hinges, 4 miles away by straight line, but 6 by road, I returned getting back by about 12 P.M. I was in a beastly mess! The rotten part was being unsupported. No supports were sent us, and it was beastly thinking any minute they would come but never came. They were ordered not to. Those who penetrated into the rampart on our left held on for about ten minutes and then were stripped of their equipment by the Germans, shot and thrown over the parapet. These were only a few too exhausted. Several men came back and told us that. It was truly wonderful. Here one Battalion had in part succeeded when a whole _____* had failed in the morning. The Colonel has been praised by all the other Colonels and Generals for what the Battalion did. Not a man hung back, all charged as far as possible. A finer set of men than these, and mostly Reservists, could not be found anywhere.

On returning I find myself in charge of a Company of 25 men instead of 200. This is temporary as Officers will soon stream out. We lost over 500 men. I feel a changed person at present and unable to laugh or smile at anything, feeling almost in a dream. Next time the Germans <u>will</u> get it. Given a chance with wire down and at close quarters, they will be slaughtered, and I feel quite mad at it, and long for a decent smash at them. I shall get the chance yet with

---

* Again the security-minded Lionel censors himself—this time when describing the strength of the attacking unit.

any luck, and I shall never forget May the 9th, 1915, a Sunday, and a marvelously clear day. You can't tell how I want to get at them and not hung up by barbed wire and the G_____ 15 yards away. I cannot write any more as I feel tired, so please excuse an absence of letters for a week.

I cannot write Father yet or anyone else so perhaps you will copy this for him. I should like you to send a copy to Mr. Pemberton. If he sees the casualty lists and hears of the fighting he might wonder.

I trust you will write other relations for me. I will do so by degrees. Must end now, feeling very tired.

> Your affectionate son
> Lionel Sotheby

~

14 - 5 - 15

My dear Mother,

Many thanks for your letter. You must not expect many letters for it is impossible to write now almost. Perhaps you will explain to Father to whom alas I have not written for ages.

Despite our losses we are at it again, having received slight reinforcements. Every man is needed now and I don't know how it will end. On that awful day I lost my auto strop safety razor & have no shaving material now, could I have one as soon as possible?

Could you also send my other <u>khaki jacket</u> sent home long ago. It is urgently needed. The casualties out here are awful, & weather is cold with rain again.

P.S. Need some more lavatory paper.

> Your affectionate son
> Lionel

~

May 15th, 1915

[unaddressed]

Our casualties were roughly 500. Despite our losses we are up again, being reinforced by 200 men and 2 officers. More to follow. I commanded D Coy. and C Coy. respectively for 6 days, 1 Company for 4 days, the other for 2 days, but I have no wish to be anything than a second Lieut. out here—one is part of the men themselves then, and that is what I like. You must please not mind few letters, as writing is well nigh impossible at times, and it needs great concentration to be able to write at all as one is in such a whirl. I only hope that if I do fall it will be in such a charge as on Sunday, May 9th, for the Colonel has got the praise of all the Brigade, and General Munro of the Division came and specially thanked the Regiment. On Thursday I was asked to give details of the ground etc. The Prince of Wales and 3 others were present. I found the Prince very nice to talk to, though he seems awfully young. What's going to happen I know not, whole regiments get wiped out, yet up they go again.

[unsigned]

∾

1st Black Watch
1st Division
24 - 5 - 15

My dear Mother,

Many thanks for your letters. I am at present in need of tooth powder, <u>very hard</u> brush for cleaning clothes, boot-brush, writing paper, & a <u>small</u> but very sharp knife for cutting pencils.

Magazines, novels & weekly papers are needed in abundance because the men enjoy them so also.

I also enclose a khaki jacket which wants mending & then to be returned. Inside the coat will be found a package, this contains some French cartridges (rifle). They are quite safe to handle & will only go off if you place them in a fire or hit them very hard with a hammer or some other object, or still more unwisely they will go off if fired from a French rifle so you see they are not very dangerous if these 3 points are kept into consideration. I enclose the "Black Watch" cap-badge of Lce. Cpl. Swan, who was shot dead through the head when we were lying down in front of the Bosches' parapet on the 9th. He was a foot away on the left. The explosive bullet ploughed a hole big enough to put your fist into, in his forehead, eventually coming out and hitting a side of his cap badge. I took his cap which was blown off practically on to me, and divested the badge by judicious manipulation underneath me. Even then I was on the lookout for souvenirs. I value the article enormously and will always keep it in remembrance of "that day."

I have completely recovered my spirits again, due I think to our huge reinforcements of 380 men and about 20 officers, 4 are coming to-night. We are stronger than ever and have been in the trenches since the 14th. We have another month to do before we get our week's rest now. Attacks occur every day. We have moved south and now with the French. They attack day and night.

Tremendous bombardments for 2 continuous hours. On the left to the North the German counter-attack lost ground. The losses on both sides are appalling.

We are in real trenches here. They are in chalk and absolutely no cover. Our communication trench is <u>1 mile and a quarter</u> and takes 55 minutes to penetrate! The ground is slightly high and we get mercilessly shelled, worse than Richebourg. 1 shell yesterday killed 4 and wounded 3 alone.

I am afraid the war will last long yet, but in a <u>month's time</u>, or anyhow <u>two months</u> we shall get well on the move. Italy has now come in and reinforcements from Germany will be given to Austria. *I am sure Germany is at the top of her power and when you can go no higher you must come down. Were we to know it, I believe Germany is practically over that crest, and will soon descend. Do not think the descent will make joy days of it for us, far from it, the bloodiest and the worst fighting will then take place, and advance will be slow, but victory is coming, we are all confident out here. Our men are of fine physique. Only 5 of my old platoon are now with me, but the new members look even better than the others. All have been out before and wounded.*

Weather tremendously hot now. Saturday night 11 P.M. till 2 A.M. was an awful thunderstorm which hung overhead without moving and the lightning was incessant. The French attacked on the right bombarding for 2 hours first. On the left we attacked (not this regiment). We had to hold the enemy. The sight baffled all description. The incessant flash of gun and lightning and the intense ear splitting noise of the guns and thunder, and then the rockets going up, made a scene too wondrous to believe. I enjoyed it immensely, and have never felt more joyful before as in the last days of last week and now.

Must end now as have no time for writing hardly. I hope Grandma is alright. I find it impossible to write much in these eventful days, but as you always pass on letters an atonement in part is made.

Nigel too wrote me a letter which I have been unable to thank for yet. [Aunt] Hennie sent me some fruits and cake, will you please thank her for me, I am unable to. Also Aunt Barbara for her foodstuffs & cigarettes, which I much enjoyed.

Must end now,

> *Your affectionate son,*
> *Lionel*

---

* Italy joined the war on 23 May, the day before Lionel wrote this letter. Lionel hopes that the diversion of German troops to bolster Austrian forces against Italy will allow the Allies to "get well on the move" on the Western Front.

May 26, 1915

Dear Mr. Sotheby,

I have just had the privilege of reading a splendid letter written by Lionel to a friend at Eton, who has sent it on to me. It is the best written & most graphic account of the splendid bravery of our Army that I have seen, and the deeds of that awful 9th May. I have no doubt you have also heard it all: and I thank God for your own sakes that Lionel has pulled through. The moral of it is perfectly clear: to send our men up against entanglements with only shrapnel behind them is to murder, and it appears that the supply of high explosives is wanting. I shall probably be at Carnarvon one day this summer on business connected with my farm. If I had time I should like to come over to see you for an hour or so. Is there any chance of your being at home? What has happened to Nigel?

> *Believe me*
> *Yours sincerely,*
> *P. Williams*

Dear Mr. Sotheby,

Your letter dated the 21st May reached me here this morning and I was delighted to hear news of you and Lionel.

What a grand little fellow he is, and if you will allow me to say so, we are full of admiration for <u>your</u> splendid energy & enthusiasm also.

We had not heard of Lionel for what seemed to be quite a long time, & both my wife and I were beginning to fidget, so your letter was doubly welcome. She wrote him a long chit-chat on the 24th.

Out of 14 he was the only officer that escaped. Heavens! What a scene this conjures up to the imagination!

With such experiences I fear Lionel will be an old man by the time he returns to England, but it is worth being born to possess such a son as that. I only hope my boy Mordaunt turns out one quarter as well, & I shall thank God for it, & be grateful.

My wife has thirty relations serving at the present time abroad either in the fighting line, the Navy, or in one capacity or another in connection with the war. Every single member of my family of fighting age is serving with the sole exception of some Spanish nephews I have, who are of course not English, & do not speak English even. You may rest assured the Sotheby trio are <u>daily</u> in our thoughts.

> *Sincerely yours,*
> *W. A. Pemberton*

May 30, 1915

Dear Mr. Sotheby,

Please excuse delay. The letter is supremely interesting & gives a marvelous picture of your boy's pluck & keenness, though he has said nothing to advertise himself. You may well be proud of him. The news I get of the Etonian officers is certainly splendid.

If I may keep this letter please don't trouble to write—but if you wish to have it returned, a post card will recover it. I do trust he may come back all right, & his brother too.

Yours very truly,
E. Lyttelton

10 More Narrow Escapes

June 1915

June 7

My dear Mother,

    In great hurry. Some more "lemon stuff" wanted. Indeed in this hot weather one needs a constant supply of it. I also want a small bottle of Morphia pills. I lost my last.

Your affectionate son
Lionel

~

15 - 6 - 15

My dear Father,

    I am quite well. The weather is tremendously hot & the flies and blue-bonnets here are plagues.* Thousands fly before one when going along the trenches. We have been in these trenches 6 days & never know when we are going to attack. This place has been fought for many times & quantities of Germans & British lay about unburied, chiefly behind our lines when we drive them back.

    At time of writing there is a great deal of heavy shelling on both sides, so I can't write much. Must end now.

Your affectionate Son
Lionel

---

* Lionel probably means bluebottles, flies that deposit their eggs in carcasses or wounds.

June 15, 1915

My dear Mother,

Many thanks for your letter & Aunt Dodie's & all the parcels received; they are immensely enjoyed.

The pest of flies here at present is awful. Could you send some fly papers? I am afraid it is due to the dead bodies lying about. The flies will bring disease sooner or later. The stuffs you have been sending from Tunbridge Wells are better than those from Home Stores. The Café au lait was very good in the early mornings.

I must end now.

Your affectionate son,
Lionel

∼

June 17, 1915

My dear Uncle Bootie and Aunt Hennie,

Many thanks for your different letters and Magazine which arrived yesterday.

My wonderful good luck continues.

After having served 6 days in the firing line of trenches in a nerve-racking spot, called _____, where a slight advance was carried out yesterday & the day before, this company was then placed in the Support trenches 100 yards back where we got all the worst shelling with lamentable results. On Tuesday we delivered one of the heaviest bombardments I have yet witnessed. It was not the amount of guns firing, but the size of them which impressed one. The shells were immensely powerful being mostly fired from 11 inch guns and were exactly the same as the German Jack Johnsons. Such a number of heavy ones fired by us has never been done before and it proves our ammu-nition is bucking up. We have always had to listen to the German ones, but now we seem to have some. Although many more were fired on May 9th & at Neuve Chapelle by us, those actual shells were mere pip-squeaks compared to those on Tuesday and Wednesday. Columns of black smoke and yellow smoke would suddenly spurt up in one dense cloud at least 40 or 50 feet and the crack absolutely deafened one. It was absolutely music to one's ears, hearing them and knowing that for the most part they were British. Of course so much fighting is always taking place at this spot the Germans had plenty of heavy artillery opposite, and naturally replied with vigour, one of their shells was said to have wiped out 50 men of _____ just on our left. Their high explosive shrapnel is beastly as we have always found out. It can either explode high up by "Time" or by "percussion" on the ground. Its radius of death is fearful and it bursts with a peculiar but terrifically loud crack which emits a deep yellow smoke. I think it is one of the most unnerving of all shells. So terrific is the explosion that at 40 feet up, each shrapnel bullet makes a hole as big as a cricket ball in the ground. It contains over 400 bullets usually. Their favourite plan is to burst them 3 together at a distance of 100 yards apart about 8 yards off the ground—without cover no one can survive, and even with it the bullets search everywhere as they fly backwards and in every direction, while the explosion is sufficient to kill one sometimes. But most of this you will see written in the Daily Mail side articles occasionally.

Well, on Tuesday afternoon this very heavy bombardment started, and they shelled us back particularly by the railway, as they thought we were bringing up reinforcements. We lost several men and some machine gunners. Four very heavy French shells fell short between our front line and support trenches. Luckily no one was hit.

The wind was North East and the smoke and fumes from all these shells was beastly as it blew our way. It made quite a fog, though not such a one as on May 9th. After about half an hour the shells fell less thickly and we heard heavy rifle fire; the bullets zipped over the embankment but were too high for us to suffer from them. It is surprising what a quantity of rifles blaze at one even after a heavy bombardment.

The results of the charges I will not write because there are facts which perhaps had better not be mentioned. It was during this time that my Company Officer asked me to find out from Captain Forrester[*] who was up in the front line on the left of the embankment, how things were proceeding. I took my runner, and we set forth. Although the German shrapnel was bursting incessantly it is surprising what little damage they do in the trenches. We at last reached the front line where I saw Captain Forrester. We looked along the line at our backs and saw the shrapnel bursting everywhere. Its effects could be seen by the dust spurting up, but it seems to me very useless stuff having no "blow back." Indeed if it had a "blow back" no one could have existed in that breastwork where we were.

From this height we were able to look down at the attack just on the other side a few yards away. It had by this time fizzled out I think for we advanced no more, and it was chiefly the Germans shelling us back all along the line at the back, where our supports were.

---

[*] Captain Robert Edgar Forrester commanded D Company.

Captain Forrester then asked me for a cigarette and when I said I thought I had not got one said laughingly "he would never let me come up into his company lines again." However I found one. He then pointed out a few things and looked over the parapet, explaining where one of our shells had blown up a German machine gun emplacement on the embankment only 100 yards away. We both looked at the spot for barely 5 seconds and our heads could barely have been 6 inches apart when I was suddenly knocked over from the parapet step by Capt. Forrester, who fell like a log into the small 1 foot deep trench below. I had heard a great crack which the German bullet makes at close range, and so knew what had happened. There he lay at my feet, a great hole behind the left eye, his eye shot out and most of his brains hanging out, a great stream of blood rushing out. The bullet had come out the other side of the head and must narrowly have missed me too.

The poor fellow never moved. The bullet must have pierced some arteries for I have never seen such a stream of blood before, it ran down the shallow trench right down the embankment for many yards and formed a ghastly pool which looked almost black.

The poor fellow shuddered once or twice, but I think it was only his muscles contracting. We tried to place his brains, at least I supposed that peculiar lump of white things was brains, into that great hole, which was large enough to place 4 fingers together, and then tied his head up but it looked horrible as the blood continued to flow. The stretcher bearers came at length to take him away, they pronounced him dead, so death after all had been very swift and painless.

Captain Forrester was one of the nicest men in the Battalion. A Regular Officer and greatly prized for his abilities. He was indeed an absolutely perfect Officer, and for a man to go like that makes it seem almost like murder. He had curly hair and was very handsome, and to see him lying in his blood was an awful spectacle made worse by the clearness of the day.

It was an extremely lucky escape for me again, for had the sniper, as I believe it was, selected myself, who was 6 inches to the right of him, it would have been different.

Somehow a little episode like that has a great effect on one, and despite how callous one is sometimes these things touch one deeply.

I went back afterwards to my own line. The next day, that is, yesterday, had yet another escape. Our kitchen was being prepared for us so as to have it at 1 o'clock. Everything was laid. The others had gone outside as some heavy shells had burst about a hundred yards away. Suddenly the Germans shortened their range and a shell fell right through our mess dugout scattering the lunch everywhere and burying everything. It was an awful mess. My servant after the shelling retrieved my knife which I keep now as a souvenir as the bone handle has been blown off, the metal inside twisted and the blade dented. All other property was lost.

That was a near escape for all of us, as Hay, the Company Officer, myself, Merrilees, Mitchell and White all mess there together, and it would have been a clean wipe-out.

That was not the only shell which fell short of their previous ones. They placed seven more and the damage this time was worse. We lost 5 killed and 9 wounded.

One shell fell close to our Sergeant Major who was going to put up a notice for a trench. He heard the shell coming, crouched against the trench, but it burst only 10 yards from him, and the poor chap received most of the effect of it. I won't describe his condition. The other shells buried several and a piece of one entered a dugout and tore one man's side clean away. He died without a murmur, I believe. Until we pulled him out, they thought he had died of heart disease, because he looked uninjured. It was heart trouble in a sense because the piece of shell must have entered that organ. The other two fellows we dug up after at least 10 minutes from their entombment. They were a ghastly sight from not being able to breathe. The explosion and pieces of the shell had also wounded them badly. They were practically dead, and died soon after. Another man received from one of the shells a large piece right into his stomach, it doubled him up, and made him feel ill. He too will die, I am afraid.

We did not receive any more shells in that particular place, but it disturbed our rest. I was exceedingly hungry that evening as I had no breakfast, having had a headache at the time, and then our lunch was blown away.

The flies here are simply terrible, huge hordes fly before one when one walks about. Quantities of dead lay about unburied and the stench in places is fearful. This part of ground has been won and lost many times and people cannot be buried for the most part.

I explored an old German trench with Merrilees on Sunday and we discovered quantities of dead Germans and others half buried with only the boots sticking up. We looked for souvenirs, but the odour was too great to allow of one approaching too close.

Mines are the great drawback here as one never knows when they are going up. The Germans exploded one on Tuesday, but it was too premature, and blew most of their own trench in. However they blew one up in our lines the day before we came in, blowing up over 100 men and many sappers. There is something wrong about these mines. We have several finished now, but we are not allowed to blow them up yet. The Germans are mining too, and it is dangerous not to blow up one's mine when completed as was shown by that one the other day. Ours was finished and the Germans came across (under) and blew it up for us—"They had," said an enquirer to me, "many galleries leading off from their main tunnel; because the explosion which resulted was too great to have originated from less than two galleries."

I have seen the crater, it is enormous. Fully 60 feet deep and with water at the bottom. It is about 50 yards wide by 150 yards in length and looking into it, is like looking into a volcano, our trench now runs behind it. The earth has been thrown to a height of at least 30 feet from the normal level, and one can see right into the German lines, and see them moving about, but we are not allowed to fire from this position, because the engineers do not wish another mine to be disclosed.

I went down one of these mines the other day. They are very eerie. There is a shaft about 40 feet deep, with a rope ladder attached. Above is a huge pump worked by two men to keep the water down. At the bottom on the right there is a small tunnel 3 feet high and 3½ feet wide supported with rafters and beams. This leads about 150 yards to a rise up, of about 5 feet, where the tunnel branches to the left and right another 100 yards or so. Here the air is very foul and the sides of the tunnel drip with moisture. At each end there is a little recess made, and a hole about 6 inches in diameter is bored 12 feet into the solid earth. Here we have to place men to listen for the enemy mining or counter-mining. The men have rifles or bandoliers only, in case the Germans break through. It's very nervy work, especially as we know the Germans are mining all along the front but the men stand it very well.

Must end now. When you have finished with this letter you might send it on to Mother to keep as it is quite impossible to keep a diary, and letters are just as good.

Your affectionate nephew,
Lionel

～

24 - 6 - 15

My dear Mother,

Many thanks for your letter. The lemon drinks have come in abundance & I have enough for the next month at least. The puttees have not come yet.

A shell buried all my cooking & eating utensils just before my lunch the other day. Could you send me another knife, fork & spoon (all separate) & 2 plates as soon as possible.

We are now having 7 days' rest.

I wrote a long letter to Aunt Bootie the other day which you will get soon.

We are absolutely full with work, so must end now. Will write you a proper letter sometime.

Your affectionate son,
Lionel

~

28 - 6 - 15

My dear Mother,

They have actually sent my name in for Leave again. It goes in on July 1st so if I get [it] I shall come back on July 2nd or 3rd. I suppose they consider I need some after the recent heavy fighting of May 9th. It is my completion of 6 months' service out here on the 30th, a longer service than is granted many. Indeed every Captain & all the subalterns are different to those at the end of last April.

I never expected leave at all, as it's very unusual to get it 2½ months after one's last leave. Of course I may not get it, though. You might ask Mrs. Lloyd to forgive my not sending her a shell nose. I have really been too fed up with shells since May 9th to dig them up especially as we have had to do chiefly with Jack Johnsons & their noses weigh too much. So I will dispose of a German cartridge un-fired instead until I get enough energy up to dig for noses.

General Haking said to both Merrilees & myself that we ought to get leave. That was on an inspection the other day after coming out of the trenches & he noticed us especially having seen us twice before on inspections for him. You need not send anything to London this time as things are so uncertain.

I received the Puttees & cigarette case alright. Also the fly papers, etc. Must end now.

Your affectionate son,
Lionel

11 Ambushed in a Listening Post

27 July–23 August 1915

Lionel has just returned from Leave.

29 - 7 - 15

My dear Mother,

I arrived here safely on Wednesday [July 28]. As regards that bomb I left behind, I feel uneasy about it, in case it went off, by accident of that case falling into the fire, or falling down. As I am not there I should not like to miss its explosion, so I would ask you to place it in a box or something in the <u>cellar</u>, placed in some place where perhaps it will not be touched, perhaps the damp will dampen its ardour of going off. The inside pieces can be kept however in the drawing room as there is little chance of them going off; they containing nothing explosive. I hope you will confer to [comply with] these suggestions as soon as possible.

My train 7:15 P.M. from Victoria on Monday was altered to 5:40 P.M. I missed & went on the next day by the 8:30 A.M. I arrived Boulogne at about 12:30 noon. There I saw Father, who after much trouble managed to get permission to drive me to St. Omer, but no further. I found there were no trains up to the front till the next morning at 5 A.M. At 3 P.M. we motored & arrived at about 7 P.M. after a most glorious spin. We put up at hotel & then found my train left at 3:25 A.M. next morning. Father saw me off most kindly, & I journeyed by train the next 25 miles. I then had to walk up to the trenches & at length found the regiment billeted ½ mile behind the trenches. This was 10 A.M. We went into the trenches at 4 P.M. & are in now.

We are in a very badly shelled place indeed, & in one place only 15 yards from the Germans across a crater (from an exploded mine). This is the nearest I have been yet. Bombs of all kinds fly over all day & the casualty list last night was 2 sergeants killed and 3 men severely wounded. All from bombs. One bomb fell at the feet of one sergeant blowing both legs off & killing him instantly. We seem to like getting near the Germans, because all the sap heads running about 100 yards from the original fire trench, have been linked up by digging from them on either sides. Thus we are getting nearer the Germans than ever. Soon we shall use each others' parapet & take turns at firing over it, as once depicted by Punch. This is a beastly place for bombs & shells. They have sent over quantities of pip squeaks in my direction all day, as they see some of the results of my digging operations during the night. Another draw-back is the lack of dugouts.

We have lost 2 Officers since I went away, one by name Garden was badly wounded.* The other our chief bomb officer was blown up by one of his own bombs.

His name was George Mitchell, an amateur boxer, from whom I got the b____s. He was with one of his big bombs & the time fuse went wrong, when practicing with it. Result, the bomb went off, blew him to pieces, also killed several men. One corporal was badly wounded, & will die, & many others were wounded. Poor Mitchell was buried behind the line, not intact, because they could not find one leg & one arm.

The disaster occurred when the Battalion were having 5 days' rest, 2 miles back, & they were only practicing with bombs. They say the mess was frightful. Several people a long way away were as covered with blood & pieces of flesh, that when they returned, people thought they were really wounded.

I am feeling rather tired curious to say, perhaps because this is a very arduous place. Oh! I forgot to say, they shelled us heavily as were about to enter the communication trench. We took cover, which was lucky as several shells actually landed on the route. A small piece made a small hole in my burberry which I was carrying. I am unable to write any other letters at present.

I have just heard that I am changed to the 2nd Black Watch, so my address will always now be 2nd Black Watch, 21st Brigade, 7th Meerut Division, Indian Expeditionary Force. Could you let everyone know of my new address as soon as possible?

Your affectionate son,
Lionel

---

* 2/Lt. J. Garden was wounded accidentally 17 July 1915, recovered, and rejoined the regiment in June 1916.

A scout on the left found 10 rounds of German ammunition & says he saw a German retiring.

Evidently our shelling has put fear into them now for they seem quite quiet. Every night now, having discovered their advanced trench, I suppose we shall have to patrol it as well, though it is only 30 yards from their ramparts & a bare 2 feet deep. I shouldn't be a bit surprised if they didn't attack our listening post with about 20 men another night as a reprisal. However I believe we shift ½ a mile or so to left in a few days so we may escape the unpleasantness.

We had some fun today, as some men on the left discovered with the aid of a periscope a large muzzle protruding over the top of the German parapet. An artillery officer came and declared it to be a pom-pom,* said he would range on it. Accordingly he ranged on it & his shells fell everywhere, over-falling only 15 yards in front of our parapet, but as these registering shells only emit smoke they are quite safe. He then put 5 lyddite shells (4.5 [inch]) over and a curious thing happened, after each shell, a German on the left jumped up showing his head, shoulders, & chest. He did this after each shell had been fired & though several of our fellows sniped at him, they missed each time.

The gunner failed to score a direct hit after 5 lyddite & about 12 registering shells, & said he would try again in the afternoon at 5:30 so we shall see some fun yet perhaps.

He also says his gun has an inaccuracy of 60 yards, & that is what makes it so difficult to score a direct hit. Machine guns are also going to open fire at the same time, so perhaps we shall also get our man with the bounce as well. It looks like rain again now but is very warm.

The "Daily Mail" still comes through the 1st Black Watch. It needs to be redirected by Smith or whoever sends it out now. I also need 100 cork-tipped cigarettes. Must end now.

> Your affectionate
> Son
> Lionel

---

* Outdated 1-inch calibre Maxim machine gun named after the sound it made.

My dear Father and Mother,

I am just beginning to settle down in this Battalion now, though it is greatly disappointing, as I have, as it were, to start all over again, get to know new people, without past services noted.

They were very surprised in the 1st Battalion when the telegram came from the base, that I was to join the 2nd forthwith, & were very sympathetic, as when one has thoroughly got to know a regiment, it's rotten being posted without reason. Apparently I was posted to the 2nd Black Watch in January. When I took that draft up at the end of the month, when the 1st Battn. had been cut up I was taken over by them as also my draft. They thought it was alright, & no enquiries were made at the base, except one when they asked on what authority I joined the 1st B. W. That was in March, & nothing more happened until Thursday, when they suddenly ordered me to the 2nd B.W. for no apparent reason as that Battalion is almost full up & the 1st is not. Accordingly I went & I am here now.

Luckily there are about 5 Etonians, two, Hastings & Brodie I know very well.* Hastings was at P. Williams with me.

When you write to any friends you might mention my new address. The Daily Mail will want re-directing also. The weather is quite warm again now. Must end now.

> Your affectionate
> son,
> Lionel

~

7 - 8 - 15

My dear Mother,

Many thanks for your letters and Aunt Dodie's. I received Mrs. Dixon's cake & it has been much enjoyed by all the officers of A Co'y, which company I am temporarily in command of. Will you please thank Mrs. Dixon for so kindly sending the cake as I doubt my having a spare moment in the ensuing times.

Times are moving now and I expect the papers will have plenty to talk about on our front within at least 3 weeks if not sooner, so you will understand a slight dearth of letters in the immediate future.

---

* 2/Lt. E. H. Rawdon-Hastings, evacuated to a hospital on 7 September 1915, died a week later. 2/Lt. E. M. Brodie, evacuated to a hospital 24 August 1915, subsequently recovered.

The Germans cheered and shouted lustily on Thursday afternoon. They put up flags on their parapets & wrote inscriptions denoting Warsaw had fallen!* We answered with rifle fire.

Must end now as the light is failing.

Your affectionate
son,
Lionel Sotheby

~

13 - 8 - 15

My dear Father & Mother,

Many thanks for letters received. We are having quite an exciting time with our listening posts this time. The enemy are about 370 yards away here, & we have listening posts in between the lines about 150 yards from our lines. I have one of these posts, was attacked the other night. This is a little diagram of the listening post. A line of willows and ditch runs out from our line & then turns at right angles to the left. Parallel to this is a narrow sap, about 4 yards from the line of willows. Along this sap, about 30 yards out on the right hand side is a small semi-circular sandbag shelter. This is the resistance post & where I post 3 men. Further on 150 yards altogether is my advanced listening post of 1 n.c.o., a bomb thrower, & 1 bayonet man. Here there is a small traverse & the sap runs on another 30 yards to a shallow trench which the Germans have converted out of a ditch. This trench is sometimes occupied by the Germans, & is about 300 yards long parallel to their front rampart. There is wire in places. This we found out afterwards.

I was proceeding from our lines down the sap to relieve the "day listening post" at 8:45 P.M. I had with me my observer & the 3 men who are on the night picquet for holding it. By some oversight I forgot to take my revolver, & only had my walking stick. When about 10 yards from the post, we were challenged loudly. We answered & on reaching the sentry I rebuked the sentry rather loudly myself, because he shouted at us.

At the same time we heard rustling in among the willows 7 yards behind us, also rustling on the right. The sentry had only time to tell me that we were practically surrounded, when the Germans suddenly opened fire. They were

---

* The German Gorlice-Tarnow offensive, under Field Marshall August von Mackensen, had captured Przemysl and Lemberg in June, and as the drive continued, the Russians evacuated Warsaw on 5 August. By the end of the month all of Poland was in German hands.

---

barely a few yards away & I was absolutely in the dark as to how many there were. How they missed our heads is a miracle, but I suppose their own nervousness & the darkness made them shoot high. I ordered my men to fire 2 rounds rapid to the left & front & then told the bomber to throw a bomb. He however in his fright had lost his bombs, & as we were all massed together, & the enemy might have thrown a bomb at us any minute, in which case he would have wiped us out, I told my men to scatter down the trench at 10 yards interval. This we did. I then sent a man back for more bombs & by the time he came back 3 minutes had elapsed without the enemy firing again. We then threw 3 bombs among the willows & also patrolled a little distance up the sap beyond our post, but as they could fire down our trench from the other end, returned back to the post.

Afterwards I put an extra two men out amongst the willows to stop any party outflanking us in the future. And so the attack ended.

There can be no doubt that they intended to cut off our advanced listening post, but the arrival of unknown numbers of us coming up the trench made them alter their plans, after they had fired upon us. If we had arrived 10 minutes later we should probably have found the post occupied by the Germans, & they could have killed all of us by simply firing down the trench sap, which is absolutely straight.

Those two men told me afterwards that they saw the Germans crawling forward a long time before we came, but did not know what to do, & lay quiet until too late. For the remainder of the night the Germans sniped back at our post from their advanced trench, often just hitting the top of our traverse. I always now have a left-flanking post in the willows to prevent a surprise from the side.

The next night at 12 midnight we withdrew the listening posts in order to shell the Germans. 12 trench mortars were arranged in our ramparts & 50 trench shells were sent over in their advanced trench. A 4.7 [inch] battery which had ranged on the German trench during the day, put several lyddite shells into the same area.* The Germans retaliated by firing back at us, but we believe they left the trench after the shelling, because last night I went with Major Wauchope† & the scouts & found nobody in their trench in front of us.

---

* Lyddite was one of the more common high explosives used by the British. It contained picric acid (a trinitrophenol).

† Major A. G. Wauchope, D.S.O., wounded in December 1914 at Festubert, commanded various companies in the 2nd Battalion and was to take command of the battalion on 6 September 1915, a command he was to hold until the end of the war.

Dear Elaine,

It is exceedingly good of you remembering my birthday & sending me some cigarettes. I shall much enjoy them, & only smoke 2 a day in order to make them last longer than others. I am "creepy-crawly" again, as we are 16 days in the same ramparts without having come out once, & consequently resting in moisture-laden dugouts with dirty straw has had the usual effect. The whole time has been & is still one long & successive period of thunderstorms. No sooner has one gone than another appears. The ground is soaked & dirty. But still I am in the best of spirits & perfectly satisfied with my lot out here.

I expect most of us here will either be back wounded or never come back at all by the end of another 2½ months, for I believe after the Germans have launched on us a terrific blow & failed presumably, we are going to attack. He who can withstand two upheavals of such magnitude will be difficult to find, nay impossible amongst regular battalions & of subaltern rank.

I was most fatigued the other night. Money had to be drawn from M_____ town [Merville] to pay certain men going on leave. M_____ town is about 14 kilometers distant. I was detailed to ride there. A bike was given me & I set out on a pouring wet day with thunderstorms. Being tired from the trenches, a beastly head-wind blowing, deep mud on the roads, I was 2 hours going & drew 1750 francs. In Merville, finding the road a little better, & it being the end of my journey, I sailed round a corner & ran into two motor convoy wagons which had smashed up. They gave me no warning. My leg was much damaged at the knee & I lost much blood, however the bike having only lost the mudguard & several spokes, still had enough energy left to make the wheels revolve. I got bandaged up & returned very tired & more. Remember I was only garbed in a kilt, which is not a bicycle costume. On getting back after cycling 28 kilometers I was very tired. You must remember it was an army bicycle & that is a solid animal resembling a traction engine & at times the mud was so thick & the bike so heavy that I made very little progress indeed. Well after handing in the money I went to rest & wash if possible. I could not eat as the strain of cycling had taken away all hunger. After a quarter of an hour the Adjt. sent for me & told me I was 300 francs short. The cashier must have overlooked one chit. He told me I must go back at once & rectify it, as the cashier left for Boulogne at 4 P.M. I felt done up but such is discipline that I said nothing but felt finished. I trundled the old wheels back again & nearly fell off dozens of times. I will not dwell on those other 28 kilometers as the road made me walk many times as otherwise I should have

AMBUSHED IN A LISTENING POST

fallen off. So much did I abhor the roads that I did the last 6 km by the side of the canal on a path 4 feet wide as the road was too much for me. The canal path is marked dangerous as so many people tip over. However I was past caring. The cashier man was just leaving his office as I raced up nearly knocking him over as the brakes refused to act. (N.B. I have always had many little mistakes with bicycles.) However I reached the trenches safely about 6:30 P.M. very tired, sore, & fed up with the 300 francs. I was unable to get any sleep as I believe it was over-tiredness. The next day came & the supposed German attack & we had much anxiety.

Must end now as am dead tired. Will you please send this letter on to Nigel, H.M.S.Brittania, North Sea, as I promised him a letter & cannot write yet. He can then send it on to Menaifron, as at present can write very few letters.

Yours in . . .
Lionel

~

23 - 8 - 15

My dear Mother,

Herewith is enclosed some dirty washing, a khaki coat & some German rifle bullets picked out of the walls of houses. The dirty washing needs puri-fying as "crawly animals" have got at them. Then please return as soon as possible.

Your affectionate
Son
Lionel

12 Straining to Go

24 August–24 September 1915

SEPTEMBER 2 (THURSDAY) These few lines are written so as to resemble a small diary in which facts are related which happened in the interim of our going into the trenches on August 24th after 6 days' rest, & the battle which is going to take place any day.

We left La Gorgue on August 24th & marched in a burning sun to the trench ramparts on the left of Neuve Chapelle, 700 yards SSW of the small village of Mauquissart, which is in German hands, or rather was, since there is no village as only broken bricks & moaning cats are the net result of heavy shells.

I proceeded [to] the Battalion with 20 men & took over stores & listening posts for No. 1 Company. Approaching the trenches there is a mile & a half of open ground intersected here & there with the commonplace French dyke & willows. These natural features admit of no cover by day & it was not until the August that troops could approach these trenches by day. Now communication trenches 1½ to 2 miles in length lead in all directions & these trenches are traversed, i.e., zigzagged.

The Aubers Ridge overlooks all this ground. Hence the coming battle, ie., the 3rd for Aubers Ridge this year. Neuve Chapelle & Festubert were all for the same objective. The country is pitted with shell holes, big & small since March played havoc with the ground. All the country here has been fought for most keenly in March & will be again. At this particular point we drove the Germans back 1655 yards & then had to retreat 300 yards as both of us could not fire over the same parapet.

Hence we used an old German trench & built up. Now the communication trenches had passed old German ramparts. Their original 1st line, supports, & 2 reserves; 2 of the latter being converted by us into Reserves.

We have about 5 lines of trenches here & all very well connected up. The support trenches having communication trenches every 25 yards. Indeed all the arrangements are made for the great attack in a few days. Into the trenches that night came many men without the vaguest knowledge of the coming attack. Thus it was we slept with even minds.

I put up wire with 10 men who have never done it before & they were themselves together constantly. The Germans are only 300 yards away so the bullets fly quite close. A bright moon is up, luckily it silhouettes them more than us.

12 midnight order comes, our company to move 1,000 yards to the left close to the bird cage where we are 70 yards from the Germans & each of us have a mine under the other. We hand over to the 58th Rifles & Punjabis & move off.

At 8 A.M. we are newly settled and as it is dawn we stand to arms.

❧

AUGUST 26 (THURSDAY) Work continues on communications trenches. We work so hard & make the earth fly so high that the enemy's artillery observers spot. He shells us with pip squeaks & revolver guns. We decamp with one casualty—a broken spade.

❧

AUGUST 27 (FRIDAY) 4:30 A.M. I go out to explore old German trench which runs to German lines 321 yards away. I take 3 men. We examine trench & find it full of dead Germans whom we heave about to discover correspondence. They are not very od[or]iferous & allow me to take some of their buttons. I find one helmet. Mostly bones in their clothes & quantities of flies' eggs. The helmet I found contained a head, to which was affixed the body. The endeavour to procure helmet resulted in head leaving body with helmet. Great difficulty in getting rid of head. Eventually successful. Very pleased with work. At 6:45 we retire after scouting ditches & getting within 30 yards of German wire. Now have several souvenirs & am pleased.

❧

29 - 8 - 15

My dear Father

    It is now midnight and I am just off duty for 2 hours. There is little rest now and the strain is much increased due to various developments which mean a greater enforced vigilance. Yesterday I captured a German. The word "captured" is however too strong because he was a deserter & did not put up a resistance. I was at work all last night & was on patrol. In the morning from 4:30 A.M. till 6:45 A.M. I was patrolling quietly along some ditches between the lines and also along some old German trenches running to the German lines 250 yards away. Dead are strewn about & we got within a few yards of their ramparts.

I found 4 Helmets, 1 silver watch, a purse with German money in notes (15 marks), a flash lamp, 1 peculiar flat bomb, buttons different kinds galore, pocket book & quantities of German letters & postcards. This stuff I do not know how to send away.

Well, as regards the prisoner. I was just resting after coming in, & at 5 minutes to 7 A.M. I happened to look over the parapet & saw a German with rifle & bayonet rushing towards us. A sentry fired one shot & missed him. As he was alone it seemed better not to fire again, but to take him alive, so we waited to receive him as he leapt down into the trench. I thought at first he was going to turn nasty, but he didn't. I told him in German to take his clothes off & we searched him. Besides his rifle & Bayonet, he had a brand new blue grey overcoat, also a "soldat buch," or paybook, a purse with little money, a respirator* & a few letters.

He was tremendously excited & voluble, shouting out the while "bonne camarade," and "nichts kaput," or pronounced by him, "nix kaput." The expression "nichts kaput" was meant for us not to shoot him. He was most highly strung & kept on shouting at us the while. Doubtless being the journey across to us in daylight with its attendant risks helped to make him a trifle excited. He threw his clothes about, & then to demonstrate he had nothing & from his talk found out that he had been miserably fed indeed he said he had eaten nothing for 4 days except boiled grass which doesn't sound appetizing. His appearance bore out his statement of lack of food as he looked exceedingly hungry & thin in the face. He also said he was a Russian Pole & there were many others in his regiment. He gave much information of interest.

After his dis-robement I said "Ziehen Sie Ihre Kleide[r] an," which means "put your clothes on." He was still intensely voluble shouting out his joyfulness at reaching us safely as he was fed up with the Germans. The fear of being shot was large as "nichts kaput" came every 3 or 4 seconds with a wail & many motions of the body.

At length I saw fit to move him, & with 4 bayonet men proceed with him to Company H.Q. where I met the Company Commander who said I

---

* Gas mask.

had better take him to Battalion H.Q. Barstow* who is Argyll officer here & can also speak German interrogated him for a minute & then we went on down communication ramparts & trenches for 1½ miles until Battalion H.Q. was reached. During this time we passed many men & the prisoner whose name was Albert Fleischer, shouted greetings at them & "bonne camarade" followed. In between however his fear that he was being led to a firing party caused the "Nix kaputs" etc. Then he had to be soothed by remarks as "Die Engländer sind freundlich," "Sie schiessen nicht," "Der Kommandant ist freundlich," etc. [The English are friendly. They don't shoot. The commander is friendly] By this means I gained a great quantity of information from him. He said that the _____ regiments were opposite, etc., etc., etc. The following things he said I think are alright to mention here. He was the 13th Prussian regiment, chiefly composed of Russian Poles. They were chiefly fed up & wanted to stop. He said there was much dissatisfaction in Germany & few soldiers, the latter remark I doubt. He said 3 more men were going to come over if he was successful but they did not come.

He had been wounded before & had been sent to the firing line with the wound unhealed. He then mentioned a truly Hunnish thing. In order to test gas the other day, 3 men were put in a dugout together, 2 with masks 1 without. Gas was then let loose, the man without the helmet succumbed after 3 minutes & was then dragged out blue & green all over. He died in pain. The others were alright for one hour & then felt effects somewhat similar. This was a test for gas!!! He said they sometimes tested gas like this with prisoners especially the English. His respirator was a good one. He said they had gas in cylinders every 4 yards opposite us & were waiting for the wind to change to attack. Flame projectors were also there. He stated his regiment was being relieved on 2nd September by the Prussians between 8 & 9 P.M. They will probably receive a few shells from us now. He said they had 12 mines under us, & 6 saps & machine guns every 20 yards!! He lived in Silesia. Must end now. Am in frightful hurry but will continue with other things when I can but the situation makes it difficult to write.

[unsigned]

[Diary resumes] At 8.30 A.M. arrive at Battalion H.Q. with prisoner. At 9.30 A.M. arrive at Brigade H.Q. with prisoner. I then return. At 2:30 P.M. am sent to Corps H.Q. at Merville where the generals live. Much talk about prisoner,

---

* Lieutenant J. A. Barstow, M.C., was later wounded at Loos in September 1915, and again along the Tigris in April 1917.

who is really a semi-deserter being a Russian Pole. Evidence from him is conflicting & we think he is either somewhat unhinged, very excited, or deliberately sent over by Germans for some object. Anyhow prisoner "raises the wind" at H.Q., as results will show.

~

AUGUST 28TH (SATURDAY) I scout from 4 A.M. till 9 A.M. in all the ditches & old German trenches. Much valuable reconnaissance 2 German night listening posts found with remains of ammunition & bread. 11 A.M. Orders come suspend work on parapet & carry on work with communication trenches with utmost rapidity. Really we don't know what to do. Three bays all mucked up with no fire step now.* Indian sappers & engineers make holes for dugouts & place in frames. They behave just like so many children, slapping each other on the backs & then running away. Their crooning noises are very annoying when one tries to snatch 2 hours sleep out of the 24. No. I Coy, in which I am having the command of No. 3 platoon, is very short of officers, having the company commander Wilson,† who is a ranker & myself & Egerton.‡

It rains all day, trench in mess & gloomy outlook.

1 P.M. News comes that we are going to bombard enemy's positions (trenches) from 2 P.M. to 6 P.M. This due to my prisoner I suppose, as he told me that the Germans had gas ready for an attack & were only waiting for a wind. Rather a long wait for them as there have been no East winds since June 9th, if I remember right.

The bombardment starts with field guns. For 2 hours I suppose we send over about 3,000 shells, which if they do as much damage to the enemy as theirs do to us, will only knock in a few sandbags & pull up a few strands of barbed wire. At 4 P.M. we used 12 4.5 [inch] guns & they did an appreciable amount of damage. Indeed one shell fell short & hit the telephone dugout of No. 2 Company. It killed 3 & wounded 3. I inspected damage done. The men had the usual purple colour due to being buried. One had about 3 pounds of his arm taken off, a few ounces off his head & one hand. Otherwise only suffering from suffocation.

---

* Most trenches had a shelf carved out of the parapet that served as a firing platform.

† Company Sergeant Major W. Wilson, promoted from the ranks 15 June 1915. A ranker was a soldier commissioned from the ranks.

‡ 2/Lt. P. G. Egerton was wounded at Loos 25 September 1915. He recovered, only to die of other wounds received in Palestine.

Our shells did much damage & exploded 2 enemy bomb & ammunition depots in front line trench. Hundreds of bombs exploded in quick succession. Star shells ascended in hundreds including several red lights, which are sent up when artillery support is needed. Consequently enemy shelled us in return. We smashed endless barbed wire & ramparts, putting at least 10 heavy lyddite shells into the same place to assure good work.

At 5 P.M. Mother started & lobbed 35 shells over from 4¼ miles in rear somewhere near Vieille Chapelle. Great damage was inflicted to the ground between the lines as Mother who is a 9.2 inch howitzer had not got her eye in yet. She makes a hole about 25 feet wide & 15 feet deep, depending on hard or wet soil. Boulders of earth weighing 2 hundredweight & more are often sent up by these eruptions.

At her 8th shot she began to get set & laid about in fine style. A small ruined house a few yards behind fire trench was smiling in sunlight serenity one minute. In another second it had evaporated into dust, which must have choked many people. And so Mother plodded on. Now scoring a boundary by blowing enemy's parapet & wire into oblivion, & then again causing the observers & spectators on our sides to draw in their breath, as she just missed our parapet. Two more 100 pound shells were added all falling into the same nest. At last Mother came herself & all exploded together. The concussion was great & much damage was done. To end up the performance one more shell came which sent up clouds of spray from the same ditch, mingling with the fumes.

It was now 6 P.M. & performance was closed. The results were good. Our takings were good & the shooting was good. Our casualties were trifling & all the enemy's best men seemed absent as they only sent over 300 or so shells & these were chiefly pip squeaks. A few of theirs were the 4.7 [inch] high explosive & shrapnel, woofs as we call them.

The bombardment was a nice diversion & interested me immensely. Consequently a periscope was glued to my eye for 4 hours. When Mother is fired you can see the shell descending the last 100 yards & see it enter the ground. It looks no bigger than an 18 pound field gun, which proves its real size, & several feet long. Well we are fidgety; having to bombard Germans as we are afraid of them attacking.

This all due to my prisoner. He got the wind up.

10 P.M. Am very tired. No sleep again to-night & it pours with rain. Am just about to go out wiring.

AUGUST 29 (SUNDAY) 3 A.M. Am now feeling dead tired & weary. We all know now that an attack by us is imminent. Urgent orders as to work came in all the night. I received them & my valiant wiring party & I put up 13 coils of barbed wire & 15 chevaux defrise,* successfully wiring in the confluence of two ditches. It took us 3½ hours & I lost one man as they turned a searchlight on us. We are all scared of a German surprise attack & surveillance is doubled. Germans also seemed scared as they brought up 3 searchlights.

~

3 - 9 - 15

My dear Mother,

I am quite well & in the best of spirits as great deeds are about to be done, and perhaps I shall again have my usual good fortune. More it is not permitted me to say. Heavy rains have fallen the last few days & everything is dreariness. The trenches are deep in mud and water & here we are herded together in the rain mostly without dugouts. We dig all night being only a few yards back from the firing line. The rain and beastly soddenness are curiously to-day making us extremely virulent to the objectionable people over the way & makes us even more determined & longing to be up & at them. They will see. The men are stoical & indeed marvelous as despite being covered an inch in mud & up to their _____ in water, they only let out certain English abbreviations, joke & laugh, a bad omen for the G's.

Today at 4 A.M. in order to get clear of the mud & water I coated my feet & legs in 5 sandbags each. I then set out to go about 40 yards away. The effect was odd, by shuffling along I accumulated a tidal amount of mud & water which swept into dugouts & overlapped my knees; therefore I desisted after slipping up. However I am cheerful. I don't know what a billet is like now as we have not been out of the trenches for ages & mud & water is our sole companion. We have delivered & suffered minor bombardments & lost our telephone men the other day all buried & killed.

Still I have never felt more content & happy & only hope the next week or perhaps prolonged month will let me go unscathed in order to complete my year out here. However I am doubtful. My 8¼ months out here are now finished.

---

* One of several varieties of barbed wire supports.

Much has happened recently. I captured a live German of the 13th Prussian Regiment the other day. More anon. I have also done much scouting by daylight. Having dug a tunnel under the parapet I have 4 times sallied out with a sergeant of Bombs, 1 bomb man & 1 bayonet man. The tunnel leads into a ditch & from this many branch off. We have exploded all. The Germans are 300 yards away & the ditches are about 6 feet deep with little water. We usually penetrate to 20 or 30 yards from their parapet, & each time they have fired on us, preventing our going further. You see they must have heard the water splashing, the reeds moving, also we had to expose ourselves to observe their parapet & wire. However the depth of the ditch gave us plenty of cover. This reconnaissance will prove of use in the next few days.

Many dead Germans lie in these ditches till the other day not disturbed but of course a souvenir hunter woke them up as such little things as uniforms filled with bones do not affect one now. Consequently I have brought in 4 German helmets two with the Prussian eagles on them, motto "mit Gott für Konig [König] und Vaterland" with God for king & country, & the other 2 with Bavarian arms: motto, "In treue fest," strong in faith.

Also two more eagles without helmets. Buckles with "Gott mit uns," God with us, also buttons of various natures, crowns, etc., 3 watches, 1 very good cigarette case, electric lamp, 47 marks (8 shillings) in German silver & paper (notes) & many letters & postcards, & pieces of equipment etc. Will continue later as am dead tired & cold with the wet.

> Your affectionate
> Son
> Lionel

∾

13 - 9 - 15

My dear Father,

I am sorry not to have written sooner but circumstances make it quite impossible.

Will you please remember me to Uncle Herbert & also to the Commandant of the Division in Etaples. I cannot write to anyone hardly at present & you will soon understand. The weather is glorious again now, which will make it all the easier for us soon.

Instead of writing recently I have been compiling a short diary which I will send home after the show. Everybody seems very happy at present & the weather intensifies it all the more. I have sent home to Mother several German helmets & other souvenirs. I heard from Mr. Williams the other day, & will endeavour to write him next month.

There's nothing to describe as it would [be] unwise to mention things, so I will end.

Your affectionate
Son
Lionel

~

21 - 9 - 15

[unaddressed]

Well we are back in La Gorgue for the last 3 days some of us will again spend.

Some time has elapsed since last writing due to not having a single moment to spare. The work has been tremendous & slight trouble with the men has been now & then experienced. Digging has been done night & day. 3 more 2¼ mile communication trenches have been dug (6 feet deep). Dugouts innumerable have been built in firing line & hundreds of other places. Tramways of wood have been constructed, some on top of and other low down in the ground. The country is a honeycomb of trenches, dugouts, tramways & cuttings. Never have such preparations for an attack been conducted so minutely as this. But the work involved has put a severe strain on everyone.

Added to this we have been expecting to attack, to go & attack each day, & it has been postponed. Our enormous quantities of guns have thrown quantities of shells over day & night. However the event is close now & I believe Thursday or Friday will see the event.

I have never been so keen to attack as now, indeed the 9th of May experiences are blotted out before the present enthusiasm.

Everybody is straining to go, the men mostly to see the result of their toil reap some reward, & the officers chiefly because some unseen force is instilling a greater wish than ever to be at them. This is so I am sure because although I cannot define it, I feel tremendously elated at the thought of getting into their trenches.

Of course we know that previous experiences should have taught those of higher rank that it is folly to bring troops up for the attack without being schooled in the nature of the ground in front of them, as was done in many instances in the fatal 9th of May. Troops were then told to attack the German parapet, without ever knowing what lay between the lines & hundreds of lives were lost in the deep dykes & ditches simply for want of instruction.

Now it is different.

Yesterday this 21st Brigade was reviewed by Lord Kitchener near the La Bassée road close to Estaires.

His comment was "Fit for anything" & rightly too, though some of us are under strength. In the afternoon we assembled at Lyddite Lane near Guncotton Road to meet our new one-arm Brigadier.[*]

He talked to us about our attack & said we were to go as far as possible. We were led to believe that if successful it might develop into a large advance. His words for this Battalion were "If you take the enemy's front line trench, push on to the 2nd line. If you take the 2nd line, push on to the 3rd line. If you take the 3rd line push on as far as you can to the Aubers Ridge." He was very optimistic, even more so than people were on the earlier attacks, but his spirit of doggedness are great points to have in a Brigadier.

After that as all the officers & sergeants of the Brigade, 1st Black Watch,[†] 4th Black Watch, 58 Rifles & 33 Punjabis (Indians) were present the battalions marched up to the firing line in line of order along the route Guncotton Lane & to Winchester Street, which are allotted to us when we enter the trenches the night before the attack. We rehearsed it all.

This afternoon General Jacob,[‡] the Divisional commander, is going to see off all officers at the Mess. So the thing is close now. We came up to La Gorgue on Sunday & go out _____.

[unsigned]

∼

My dear Gladys,[§]

Many thanks for your letter, only just in time.

Tomorrow we attack & it's going to be the biggest battle in the world's history so the general says. We are billeted in a field now. Rain heavy last night. Bombardment has lasted 3½ days so far & is now simply terrific & we are 2½ miles back. The noise is awful & is as heavy now as at Neuve Chapelle.

We march into it in 3 hours' time & go over tomorrow. It is not halting at front line, but regiments have to go on until the end. You will hear about it soon as it is like nothing on earth.

---

[*] Br.-General C. E. de M. Norie

[†] 2nd Black Watch (Lionel's mistake).

[‡] General Sir Claude W. Jacob, commanding the Meerut (7th) Division.

[§] Gladys Farrow, a friend. This is the only letter in the collection addressed to her. The letter is undated, but must have been written 24 September 1915.

This will probably mean my return in the next few days. The smoke from the shells hangs low like a fog & everything is damp from last night's thunderstorm.

Goodby now as I must end.

Yours in . . .

Lionel

P.S. We are front line & to us falls the honour of going in trenches first.

❧

23 - 9 - 15

My dear Father,

Tomorrow morning[*] we go over the parapet and I am in the front line. I will send you a postcard if chance offers, but our position will be rather an invidious one in some respects as regards time for writing & for perhaps several days. We are all cheerful & full of hope though no one knows what is before him. The outcome of it all should be large, as superior officers have by now perhaps rectified the Boer War ways of attack.

It is going to be a cold night & the moon is up.

I have not the uneasy tremors which one experiences during the night before one's first attack, partly because I suppose the novelty has worn off, & partly because of a greater & stronger determination to come through. It is more or less the same with the men, as most of them were in the 9th of May Neuve Chapelle & do not wonder what their feelings will be like on the morrow. The general spirit of everyone is good & it bodes well for us.

Farewell for the present.

Your affectionate

Son,

Lionel

P.S. I have not written Mother.

This was Lionel's last written communication of any kind that has survived.

---

* This letter, therefore, must actually have been written on the 24th, not the 23rd.

2

23 . 9 . 15

My dear Father,

Tomorrow morning we go over the parapet & I am in support line. I will send you a postcard if chance offers, but our position unpredictable as regards winning or losing or [...] for perhaps some days.

We are in cheerful spirits & though no one knows whatin before him.

Therefore if it all should be lost [...] as before. [...] now perhaps restful the Boer are way of attack.

It is going to be all night & the moon is up.

I have not the money interest what one experiences during the night before one's first attack, partly because of [...] suppose the novelty has worn off, & partly because of [...] determination to come through.

[...] this moment is the same will [...]

[...] so must [...] too worn [...] & do not wonder what this [...] wise unlike on the moment.

The [...] of one is good & it looks well [...]

Farewell for the present.

Your too affectionate son
Lionel

THE BATTLE OF LOOS:
"ACTION AT PIÈTRE"

25 September 1915

The long-delayed Battle of Loos finally began in the early morning of 25 September, a Saturday. Loos, a twenty-mile-wide attack in Artois comprised the British share of a larger Allied offensive that also featured a simultaneous French advance on the British right. The British part of the action fell to General Haig and his First Army, whose line extended some six miles from just north of the La Bassée Canal southward to the Lens region, where the French Tenth Army extended the attack an additional twelve miles southward.

In Artois several subsidiary actions further to the north were aimed at preventing German reserves north of the Bassée Canal from reinforcing the main attack to the canal's south. Haig assigned one of these feints at Piètre to the Indian Corps opposite Neuve Chapelle and Aubers Ridge, and its commander in turn handed the task to the Meerut Division, deployed on the far left (north) of the corps's frontage. The Meerut Division's Major-General Jacob selected the Bareilly and Garhwal Brigades to lead the attack, the Bareilly Brigade forming the northern edge. In the front lines of this brigade were the 2nd Black Watch, the 69th Punjabis, and a Territorial unit of the Black Watch. Thus Lionel, in the 2nd Black Watch, No. 1 Company, found himself in the leading wave.

In lieu of sufficient artillery the British planned to rely instead on their first use of cloud gas warfare, chlorine released from cylinders and drifting on the wind, which the Germans had introduced earlier in the year at 2nd Ypres (22 April), and with which the Allies were keen to retaliate. The war diary of Lionel's battalion reported carrying and working parties practically every night in early September, though whether these fatigues were for portering pipes and cylinders into the front lines is not indicated. Gas commanders mandated the strictest secrecy with regard to these activities, and Lionel, ever conscientious, nowhere refers to this aspect of his duties at this time.

A mine under the enemy lines exploded at 5:48 and the release of a small amount of chlorine gas two minutes later preceded the jump-off just before

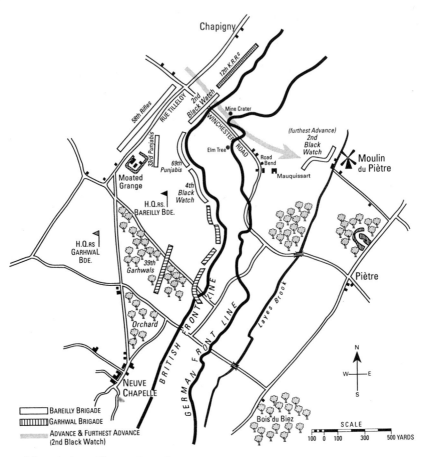

Map 5. Action at Piètre, 25 September 1915.

6 A.M. The mine obediently detonated at the depression of the plunger, but the wind proved uncertain and Lionel's battalion seems to have gotten the worst of the drifting gas. The war diary of the Meerut Division reported:

> a gust of wind came from the south east and turned the gas into our own trenches. All gas was immediately turned off, the gas detachment doing this on their own initiative, but considerable quantities entered our own trenches and caused many casualties in the 2/Black Watch on the leeward of our attack.[*]

---

[*] PRO/WO95/3931, 25 September 1915.

At 5:59 the leading platoons of the three battalions crossed the parapet, 1/4 Black Watch on the right, the 69th Punjabis in the center, and Lionel's 2nd Black Watch on the exposed far left flank. It was his unit that had to charge through the densest blanket of smoke and gas. The divisional war diary:

> On the left, the 2/Black Watch had to go through our own gas, which the wind had not been strong enough to disperse, and suffered more casualties by gassing. This battalion was not free from gas until it got into the enemy line.

The battalions went over in waves of companies, and among the four platoons of the first line was Lionel's No. 4 Platoon of Company No. 1, led by Captain Wilson. Although much discomforted by the cloud of gas, the three battalions of this leading wave of the Bareilly Brigade met with little enemy resistance, and by 6:10 had skirted the mine crater, and was in possession of the enemy's front line. Lionel's No. 1 Company had crossed and occupied the German first line near Elm Tree Salient and was moving along Winchester Road toward the Road Bend.

Finding the wire well cut by the preliminary bombardment, all three battalions pushed on, and by 6:20 had reached and occupied the German second line. By then, however, the dense smoke and gas so obscured the field of war that unit cohesion was lost, and the various companies of Lionel's Black Watch became hopelessly mixed with those of the 69th Punjabis on their right and those of the 58th Rifles, another Bareilly regiment, moving up through the confusion from behind.

Some time was lost in pulling back slightly and reforming the units. Meanwhile to their right the Garhwal Brigade, save for one regiment on its left, the 2/8 Gurkha Rifles, encountered uncut wire and were held up in front of the German front line.

By this time two successive waves of following troops were pouring out over the parapets to join in the assault. Leading the third wave was the commander of the 2nd Battalion Black Watch himself, Major Wauchope.

By 8 A.M. the various companies of the 2nd Black Watch had regrouped and were advancing on their next major target, a prominent windmill known as the Moulin du Piètre, situated just on the other side of a shallow stream, the Layes Brook, a tributary of the Lys River. The halting of the Garhwal Brigade on their right and the delay in sending covering troops from the corps on the left meant that the fast-moving Black Watch were left with both flanks perilously in the air.

The German defenders at the Moulin du Piètre were dug in effectively and though they came under intense British artillery bombardment, they managed to hold off the infantry attack. The Meerut divisional war diary contains the stark comment:

> 9 A.M. Bareilly Brigade still attacking the Moulin du Piètre.
> 9.40 2/Black Watch and 58/Rifles had captured parts of the German 2nd line, but the Germans still held the Moulin du Piètre.

The assault on the Moulin continued for the next two hours. By 9:40 all phone lines were reported lost and runners contributed the only communication. By 10 o'clock the strong point still had not been taken, but the infantry of the 2nd Black Watch hung on, lying in the shallows of the Layes Brook, waiting for reinforcements that never came. Meanwhile the Germans were massing for a counterattack. The increasingly desperate British situation during the late morning in front of the windmill is indicated by the candid war diary admission, "It is impossible to establish the hour at which these actions took place as most of the officers responsible for them have been killed or wounded."

At 11:30 an invincible German counterattack began, the exposed Black Watch right flank and then the left giving way to numerous German bombers. The Moulin du Piètre was not to be taken that day. At noon, with both flanks turned, the Bareilly Brigade was forced to retreat. All along the line the British fell back, leaving hundreds of dead, wounded, and missing in their wake. In this failed subsidiary attack, casualties in the 2nd Black Watch alone numbered 363, including 91 killed and another 271 wounded.

Among those bodies missing and never recovered was that of twenty-one-year-old 2/Lt. Lionel Sotheby. The sole bit of more explicit surviving evidence concerning the circumstances of his death is contained in one sentence in a letter written to his father by Major Wauchope, Lionel's battalion commander: "He was wounded and continued leading his men until a grenade struck him and killed him."[*] Whether Major Wauchope actually did observe Lionel's death or whether this brave and quick death reflected a not uncommon compassionate invention to console the family cannot be known.[†]

---

[*] Letter quoted in the obituary of the *Eton College Chronicle*, 21 October 1915, p. 900.

[†] Major Wauchope, in his *History of the Black Watch in the Great War* (London, 1925) misspells Lionel's family name as Sotherby.

My dear Father and Mother,

I am just beginning to settle down in this Battalion now, though it is greatly disappointing, as I have, as it were, to start all over again, get to know new people, without past services noted.

They were very surprised in the 1st Battalion when the telegram came from the base, that I was to join the 2nd forthwith, & were very sympathetic, as when one has thoroughly got to know a regiment, it's rotten being posted without reason. Apparently I was posted to the 2nd Black Watch in January. When I took that draft up at the end of the month, when the 1st Battn. had been cut up I was taken over by them as also my draft. They thought it was alright, & no enquiries were made at the base, except one when they asked on what authority I joined the 1st B. W. That was in March, & nothing more happened until Thursday, when they suddenly ordered me to the 2nd B.W. for no apparent reason as that Battalion is almost full up & the 1st is not. Accordingly I went & I am here now.

Luckily there are about 5 Etonians, two, Hastings & Brodie I know very well.* Hastings was at P. Williams with me.

When you write to any friends you might mention my new address. The Daily Mail will want re-directing also. The weather is quite warm again now. Must end now.

> Your affectionate
> son,
> Lionel

$\sim$

7 - 8 - 15

My dear Mother,

Many thanks for your letters and Aunt Dodie's. I received Mrs. Dixon's cake & it has been much enjoyed by all the officers of A Co'y, which company I am temporarily in command of. Will you please thank Mrs. Dixon for so kindly sending the cake as I doubt my having a spare moment in the ensuing times.

Times are moving now and I expect the papers will have plenty to talk about on our front within at least 3 weeks if not sooner, so you will understand a slight dearth of letters in the immediate future.

---

* 2/Lt. E. H. Rawdon-Hastings, evacuated to a hospital on 7 September 1915, died a week later. 2/Lt. E. M. Brodie, evacuated to a hospital 24 August 1915, subsequently recovered.

AMBUSHED IN A LISTENING POST

The Germans cheered and shouted lustily on Thursday afternoon. They put up flags on their parapets & wrote inscriptions denoting Warsaw had fallen! We answered with rifle fire.*

Must end now as the light is failing.

> Your affectionate
> son,
> Lionel Sotheby

~

My dear Father & Mother,

Many thanks for letters received. We are having quite an exciting time with our listening posts this time. The enemy are about 370 yards away here, & we have listening posts in between the lines about 150 yards from our lines. I have one of these posts, was attacked the other night. This is a little diagram of the listening post. A line of willows and ditch runs out from our line & then turns at right angles to the left. Parallel to this is a narrow sap, about 4 yards from the line of willows. Along this sap, about 30 yards out on the right hand side is a small semi-circular sandbag shelter. This is the resistance post & where I post 3 men. Further on 150 yards altogether is my advanced listening post of 1 n.c.o., a bomb thrower, & 1 bayonet man. Here there is a small traverse & the sap runs on another 30 yards to a shallow trench which the Germans have converted out of a ditch. This trench is sometimes occupied by the Germans, & is about 300 yards long parallel to their front rampart. There is wire in places. This we found out afterwards.

I was proceeding from our lines down the sap to relieve the "day listening post" at 8:45 P.M. I had with me my observer & the 3 men who are on the night picquet for holding it. By some oversight I forgot to take my revolver, & only had my walking stick. When about 10 yards from the post, we were challenged loudly. We answered & on reaching the sentry I rebuked the sentry rather loudly myself, because he shouted at us.

At the same time we heard rustling in among the willows 7 yards behind us, also rustling on the right. The sentry had only time to tell me that we were practically surrounded, when the Germans suddenly opened fire. They were

---

* The German Gorlice-Tarnow offensive, under Field Marshall August von Mackensen, had captured Przemsyl and Lemberg in June, and as the drive continued, the Russians evacuated Warsaw on 5 August. By the end of the month all of Poland was in German hands.

barely a few yards away & I was absolutely in the dark as to how many there were. How they missed our heads is a miracle, but I suppose their own nervousness & the darkness made them shoot high. I ordered my men to fire 2 rounds rapid to the left & front & then told the bomber to throw a bomb. He however in his fright had lost his bombs, & as we were all massed together, & the enemy might have thrown a bomb at us any minute, in which case he would have wiped us out, I told my men to scatter down the trench at 10 yards interval. This we did. I then sent a man back for more bombs & by the time he came back 3 minutes had elapsed without the enemy firing again. We then threw 3 bombs among the willows & also patrolled a little distance up the sap beyond our post, but as they could fire down our trench from the other end, returned back to the post.

Afterwards I put an extra two men out amongst the willows to stop any party outflanking us in the future. And so the attack ended.

There can be no doubt that they intended to cut off our advanced listening post, but the arrival of unknown numbers of us coming up the trench made them alter their plans, after they had fired upon us. If we had arrived 10 minutes later we should probably have found the post occupied by the Germans, & they could have killed all of us by simply firing down the trench sap, which is absolutely straight.

Those two men told me afterwards that they saw the Germans crawling forward a long time before we came, but did not know what to do, & lay quiet until too late. For the remainder of the night the Germans sniped back at our post from their advanced trench, often just hitting the top of our traverse. I always now have a left-flanking post in the willows to prevent a surprise from the side.

The next night at 12 midnight we withdrew the listening posts in order to shell the Germans. 12 trench mortars were arranged in our ramparts & 50 trench shells were sent over in their advanced trench. A 4.7 [inch] battery which had ranged on the German trench during the day, put several lyddite shells into the same area.* The Germans retaliated by firing back at us, but we believe they left the trench after the shelling, because last night I went with Major Wauchope† & the scouts & found nobody in their trench in front of us.

---

* Lyddite was one of the more common high explosives used by the British. It contained picric acid (a trinitrophenol).

† Major A. G. Wauchope, D.S.O., wounded in December 1914 at Festubert, commanded various companies in the 2nd Battalion and was to take command of the battalion on 6 September 1915, a command he was to hold until the end of the war.

A scout on the left found 10 rounds of German ammunition & says he saw a German retiring.

Evidently our shelling has put fear into them now for they seem quite quiet. Every night now, having discovered their advanced trench, I suppose we shall have to patrol it as well, though it is only 30 yards from their ramparts & a bare 2 feet deep. I shouldn't be a bit surprised if they didn't attack our listening post with about 20 men another night as a reprisal. However I believe we shift ½ a mile or so to left in a few days so we may escape the unpleasantness.

We had some fun today, as some men on the left discovered with the aid of a periscope a large muzzle protruding over the top of the German parapet. An artillery officer came and declared it to be a pom-pom,* said he would range on it. Accordingly he ranged on it & his shells fell everywhere, over-falling only 15 yards in front of our parapet, but as these registering shells only emit smoke they are quite safe. He then put 5 lyddite shells (4.5 [inch]) over and a curious thing happened, after each shell, a German on the left jumped up showing his head, shoulders, & chest. He did this after each shell had been fired & though several of our fellows sniped at him, they missed each time.

The gunner failed to score a direct hit after 5 lyddite & about 12 registering shells, & said he would try again in the afternoon at 5:30 so we shall see some fun yet perhaps.

He also says his gun has an inaccuracy of 60 yards, & that is what makes it so difficult to score a direct hit. Machine guns are also going to open fire at the same time, so perhaps we shall also get our man with the bounce as well. It looks like rain again now but is very warm.

The "Daily Mail" still comes through the 1st Black Watch. It needs to be redirected by Smith or whoever sends it out now. I also need 100 cork-tipped cigarettes. Must end now.

> Your affectionate
> Son
> Lionel

---

* Outdated 1-inch calibre Maxim machine gun named after the sound it made.

EPILOGUE

Shortly before 2 o'clock on the Wednesday afternoon of 29 September a telegram arrived at Menaifron Farm from the War Office and read as follows:

> Deeply regret to inform you that 2nd Lieut L. F. S. Sotheby A & S Highlanders was wounded and missing believed killed in action between 25/26 Sept. Lord Kitchener expresses his sympathy.

Several days later a letter arrived from the regimental Black Watch chaplain:

> *Dear Mrs. Sotheby,*
>
> *I am indeed sorry for you in the great loss which you have sustained, as I fear your son was killed in the gallant attack made by the reg't. Their work was magnificent & they captured 3 lines of German trenches before they had to come back. During this return our losses were heavy and your son may have been seriously wounded or taken prisoner, but we can only hold this out as a very faint hope. If he is dead, as we think, there is no hope of recovering his body, as he is well behind the present German line.*
>
> *The C.O. is very sorry and has asked me to send you his sincere condolences, & has hopes to write later. Please accept my very sincere sympathy.*

And from the Pembertons:

> *Dear Mr. Sotheby,*
>
> *It is hardly too much to say that if we had lost our own son, we could scarce have felt it more than we now do the loss of your gallant boy. My wife is <u>deeply</u> distressed. She was devoted to Lionel, and I can see her now, as she kissed him, when we said "good-bye;" the only man she had ever kissed in her life save her father, her two brothers—one in the Guards & one in the Rifle Brigade, killed in the South African War—and myself.*
>
> *Lionel's last letter to me was dated 24th September on eve of the great attack. He wrote always before going into action.*

He has entrusted me with a letter I was to deliver to you should he fall. I should like to give it you personally.

I was looking forward to proposing Lionel for the Carleton Club, spoke to him about it the very last time he was with us.

Great God, it is too awful to think we shall never see him again.

Yours in the deepest sympathy
it is possible for one man
to feel for another
Willoughby Pemberton

A week later Wainwright, the family solicitor, remembered the letter that Lionel had sent to him upon leaving for Le Havre back on the first day of January 1915. It had instructed Wainwright to open the sealed enclosure "in the eventuality of my going out on the ebb tide and not returning." Now he opened it and read:

Enclosure.

Perhaps these few articles, though being of no real value, will be accepted as a souvenir from one who has "fired off."

Order is nothing—all same after Mother, Father, Nigel.

To the following I bequeath—

Miss Elaine Belmont	Sphoran*
Miss Gladys Farrow	Tartan Plaid (looks like a table cloth)
Miss Violet Williams	My belt (Sam Brown)
Miss Mona Williams	Water bottle
Mrs. Pemberton	Glasses (opera glasses)
Mother & Father	To choose what they want of any of my belongings not quoted here. I would prefer that they took nothing, but remembered without need for visual objects my one time existence. Floreat Etona.
Lt. Col. & Mrs. Williams	Prismatic Compass
Wilsie	Skiendhu (kind of knife with Cairngo[r]m handle)
Mr. Pemberton	Dirk (Dress)†

---

* A sporran is a fur pouch worn in front of the kilt.
† A dagger worn with dress uniform.

| Mrs. Sotheby-Ecton | Revolver |
| Miss Williams | Glengarry |

Am tired of portioning and fed up, so other very close friends must have remnants of my military existence. I cannot think clearly for portioning up.

| Nigel, my brother, | my money deposits at Cox's about £35 |
| | Also any other effects wanted. |

Those who are closest to me I give nothing in particular, but they can have what they will. My last thoughts will be of Mother, Father, Nigel, and close friends, also Eton.

Floreat Etona.

And on 16 October a letter arrived at Menaifron Farm from Gladys Farrow.

> *My dear Mrs. Sotheby,*
>
> *Have wanted to write so much to you before to send my deepest sympathies but had heard that you had not given up hope of Lionel being among the wounded so could not write & damp any hope, altho I saw his name among the casualties. Dear Mrs. Sotheby, he was a dear brave boy and I have a letter from him written about a month ago, which I must send to you. In it he said that he had a most vivid dream, in which he saw that he would be taken in the next charge, he asked me not to mention it as it was silly perhaps to believe in dreams, but that if it did happen, that he should be killed, I was to tell you that he knew it was going to happen and was quite prepared. It will make you happy I think to know that he went with a true heart to meet God. I am enclosing a letter he wrote me on going into battle.* * *But try & cheer up dear Mrs. Sotheby, we have the greatest consolation in knowing that we shall meet those we love again, and do not think the time is far off now. With much love to you and very heartfelt sympathies, I remain*
>
> *Yours very sincerely*
> *Gladys Farrow*

Lionel was one of 1,131 Etonians who were killed in the war. On 4 June of the year he died, following an Old Etonian dinner at the Coldstream

---

* The letter Gladys mentions is not in the archives.

Headquarters at Béthune, Lionel had privately composed his own epitaph, which he confided to a sealed envelope. On the outside were the words "On my gaining still greater happiness." After his death his family broke the seal and read:

> To my Parents, School, dear Friends, and Brother: These few words are meant to embody a farewell. . . . In bidding farewell, I feel no remorse, as indeed I have been resigned to the future paved out for me by One Who knows best. . . . Think me not pessimistic; I am one who would sooner die a glorious end than live for years and die as is one's wont in ordinary life. I have been spared often, but my time will assuredly come; I sense it now. That is why I write.
>
> Eton will be to the last the same as my Parents and dear Friends are to me. . . .
>
> Never have such wonderful and heroic private soldiers assembled in such masses as today. To die with such is an honour. To die for one's school is an honour. . . . To die for one's country is an honour. But to die for right and fidelity is a greater honour than these. And so I feel it now. When it is an honour to die, then be not sad; rather rejoice and be thankful that such an opportunity was given to me. I beg of you all, mourn for me not and bewail me not, but pray. Life is but a passing image; so let it be with me.
>
> Farewell; I shall think of you all to the last, even as I think of you now.
>
> "Greater promotion there is not than promotion into the wide unknown."
>
> "Floreat Etona."
>
> "Remain ye calm and quiet, for all is well."
>
> The cables are cut and I slip away, fading into pinky mists as at early dawn, remembering you all.
>
> From beyond I call with love and affection.
>
> Farewell.

EU HABERTH NID A DEIBID · A'U HENWAU
ANNWYL NID A'N ANGD.

JOHN S. WILLIAMS, CLASFRYN.
OWEN EVANS, SHOP NEWYDD.
WILLIAM A. JONES, CLYNAFON.
LLEWELYN JONES, MAENGWYN.
THOMAS RICE, TAI TY MAWR.
EDWIN D. JONES, LON UCHAF
R. BOWEN-ROBERTS, PLAS PENRHYN.
WILLIAM JONES, TAN Y BRYN.
WILLIAM H. WILLIAMS, PEN DRE.
WILLIAM JONES, CRAIG DWEN.
DAVID WILLIAMS, TY'N COEDEN.
OWEN ROBERTS, MAES PORTH.
LIONEL F. S. SOTHEBY, MENAIFRON.
JOHN JONES, RHENC.
DAVID WILLIAMS, PENRHYN BACH.

1914 — 1918

1939 — 1945
ALUN JOHN GRIFFITH BRONALLT 32 OED
GWILYM WILLIAMS LON UCHAF 21 OED
THOMAS WILLIAMS PENRHYN BACH 21 OED

War Memorial at Dwyran, Methodist Welsh Church

INDEX

aeroplanes, German, 5–6, 7, 59; shelled, 41, 43; photographed over Burbure, 44

Amery, Capt. H. F. S., 41

Argyll and Sutherland Highlanders, xx, 61; Lionel's nostalgia for, 83; suffering of, 8; 4th Battalion, xviii; 10th Battalion, history of, xvii

atrocities (German): at Neuve Chapelle, 90; questioned, 38

Aubers Ridge, battle of, xxiii, 97–105

barbed wire: laying of, at Neuve Chapelle, 92–93, 129; laying of, at Mauquissart, 124; uncut, at Aubers Ridge, 101

Barstow, Lt. J. A., 126

baths: in Le Havre, 7

batman. *See* Keekie and Jamieson

beer: drinking, 22–23; testing, 14

Berlin, Lionel's museum visit to, 44–45

Béthune, xxi–xxii, 33, 34–38; café at, 37; its old church, 38; map, 37; shelled, 36

Beuvry, 33, 36

bicycle misadventures, 121–22

billets: at Burbure, 39–40; at Choquaux, 72; at Le Touret, 89

"Black Maria." *See* shells

Black Watch (regiment), xxi, 5, 90; Lionel's reception at, 83; parade reviewed, 67; 1st Battalion, xxi–xxiv, 17, 34; 2nd Battalion, xx, xxiv, 17, 34, 135–38; 3rd Battalion, 13n; 4th Battalion, 28

bomb (grenade) throwing: instructions, 54–55; fatal accident (February), 58–60; fatal accident (July), 116; practice, 66, 68

bombardment. *See* shelling

breastworks. *See* trenches

Brodie, 2/Lt. E. M., 117

Burbure, 38–40; Roman Catholic Church service at, 55–57

casualties: among horses and cattle, 36, 76, 89; at Aubers Ridge, 97–104; at Neuve Chapelle, 88–90, 94; in early March, 76; in early July, 116; in first division, 36

Catholic. *See* Roman Catholic

censorship: of diary entries, 39; of letters, 6; of parcels, 25; of newspapers, 20; self-censorship, examples of, 39, 102, 109, 121

Chalmer, Capt. F. G., 66

cheerfulness (Lionel's): before battle, 129, 133; characteristic, xix; despite unpleasant circumstances, 74, 121; despite dangers, 81, 93–94, 105; general expressions of, 4–5, 36, 45, 78, 80

Chocques, 32–33, 38–39

Choquaux, 74

Church parade, 49, 55–56, 63

"coalbox." *See* shells

Coldstream Guards, xv, 23, 43, 71, 76, 77, 89–91, 94

communication trench, 105, 124

complaining, *See* grousing

conscription, need for, 20

court martial, 42–43

"crime" (sheet), 31–32

Dead Cow Farm, 91–92

deserters: British, 16

deserters: German, 124–27

Duff, T. R., 28

Egerton, 2/Lt. P. G., 127

Edwards, Lt. W. H. C., 43–46, 60–64, 72

England, prevalent misinformation: about the war in general, 13, 82; about military strategy, 69; about regimental cohesion, 90–91; about subalterns, 83; naiveté, 74

equipment, list of, 73–74

Eton: Lionel at, xvii; officers from, 23, 35–36; represented in 2nd Battalion, Black Watch, 117; school casualties, 45, 141

Eton College Chronicle, xvii, 45–46, 138n

Evans, Capt. L. P., 42

Farrow, Gladys, 132–33, 140, 141
Festubert, 69
flares, 79, 92–93, 128
Fleischer, Albert (German deserter), 124–27
flies, in trenches, 108–9, 112
Flora, Mademoiselle: meets Lionel in shop, 49; visits Lionel while ill, 53
Formidable, sinking, 2n
Forrester, Capt. R. E., 110–11
Fortune, Capt. V. M., 66
Fowler, Lt. G. D., 23, 35
French (language), attempts to use, 3, 4, 9; coached by Flora, 49
French civilians: alleged cheating by, 9, 71; casualties among, 89; funerals of, 65–66; physicians criticized, 65; unreasonable demands by, 64; youngsters' misbehavior in church, 56
frostbite, 8, 79

Garden, 2/Lt. J., 116
Garhwal Brigade, 135–37
gas, employed at Loos, 135–37
German soldiers: dead, found in trench, 124; deserter (prisoner), 124–27; give notice of the fall of Warsaw, 118; intercommunication with British, 94, 97
Germany: Lionel's assessment of, 20–21, 41–42; Lionel's visit to, xviii
Gibb, Corpl., death of, 78, 80
Grant-Duff, Lt. Col. Adrian, 41n, 49
Green, Capt. W., 38
Greuze, Jean-Baptiste, 44–45
"grouse-butts," 91–92
grousing, 16, 115–16
Gurkhas, xxii, 39, 72, 82; dead, discovery of, 75; fighting at Neuve Chapelle, 90; shallow burial of, 77

Haig, General Douglas: his *Special Order*, 85; planning at Loos, 135
Haking, Major General R. C. B., 59, 60, 69; reviews Black Watch, 67–68
Haldane, Capt. J. B. S., 23–24, 66, 74; reported wounded, 88; not wounded, 90
Haldane, lord chancellor, 23
Hamilton, Major J. G. H., 38, 45, 49, 53
Harfleur, 4–35
Hart, Sergt. P., 59–60
Hay, Lt. Lord F., 64, 68, 72, 77; in command of No. 8 Platoon, 86

Hinges, 69, 72, 94

Ilford, railway disaster, 2, 2n
illness, in C Company, 53
illness (Lionel): colds, 13, 18–19, 93; flu, 49–53; stomach-aches, 75–78
Indian troops, disparagement of, 79; childish behavior of, 127; *See also* Gurkhas
Italy, joins the war, 105

"Jack Johnson" *See* shells
Jacob, General Sir Claude W., 132, 135
Jamieson (Lionel's second servant): replaces Keekie, 70; narrow escape of, 77; de-louses kilt, 95

Kedie, Capt. W. T., 86
Keekie (Lionel's first servant): dissatisfaction with, 51–53; dismissal of, 70
kilts: attractive, 36; curiosity about, 40; lice in, 95; wearing of, 3
Kitchener, 132, 139
Kitchener's army: anticipated arrival in France, 60; characterization, 16–17; integration with units, 91
kit inspection, 19–20, 55

La Bassée, 34, 38; reported capture of, 88, 90
La Gorgue, 123, 131, 132
last letter: to father, 133; to mother, 129–30
leave, 36, 114
Le Havre, xx; description of, 10–11; Lionel's arrival at, 3; map, 6; retrospection about, 58; visits to, 7, 9, 12
Le Touret, 83, 89, 90, 94
lice, 94–95, 121–22
Lillers, 34
Linette, xix, 35–37
listening post, 118–20
London Daily Mail, 84
London Graphic, 84
Loos, Battle of, xxiv, 135–38
Lowther, Brig.-Gen. H. C., 44
Lyttelton, Rev. the Hon. Edward, xvii; letter of, 107

machine guns, 42
mail: delay of, 15; need for, 83; parcels, 15; rumors about loss of, 63
malingering, 16
McFarlane, 2/Lt. R., 23, 38, 53, 66

McKenzie, 2Lt. R. I., 38, 41
marches: to Burbure, 38–40; Burbure to Valhous, 57; to Choquaux, 71–72; Le Touret to Hinges, 94
Mauquissart, 123
medicine. *See* pills
Meerut Division, 135–36, 138
Merrilees, S. B., 28, 57, 61, 63, 72, 76, 112; in command of No. 7 Platoon, 87; playing soccer, 64; sick, 75
mines, 112–13
Mitchell, George, 116
mock attacks. *See* training
morale of men admirable, 63, 82, 86, 129, 133
"Mother." *See* shells
Murdoch, 2/Lt. J., 23, 42, 49
Murray, Major J. T., 41, 42, 49; accidental death of, 58–59; burial of, 60, 61

Nash, Capt. L. C., 35
Neuve Chapelle, battle of, xxii, 81–95
Nicol, Capt., 1–4
Norie, Br.-General C. E. de M., 132
North Lancashires, 39

Orderly Officer: duty of, 13–15; Lionel as, 20, 21, 55

pacifism, scorned by Lionel, 21
Pemberton, W. A.: congratulatory letter, 106; letter of condolence, 139–40
periscope, 76, 120, 128
photographs: amateurish, 28, 29–30; missed opportunity, 44; of Sergt. McWilliams, 33; of servants and fellow officers, 74; results of, 25, 41; surreptitious, on parade ground, 67–68; taken in shop, 49; taken in church, 56; taken at the front, 39, 76, 79; terminated, camera turned in, 94
Piètre, 135–38; map, 136
pills, 52, 70–71
poetry: by Lionel, 47; quoted from *Eton College Chronicle*, 46–47; Tennyson parody, 53
pom-pom, 120
practice. *See* training
premonitions, 41, 121, 129
Prince of Wales, 104

ramparts. *See* trenches
Rawdon-Hastings, 2/Lt. E. H., 117
reconnaissance, 127, 130

reschau (portable stove): purchase of, 9; use of, 18–19, 31, 33
Richard, Lt. J. E. M., 13, 38, 42
Richebourg l'Avone, 74
rifles: damaged, 12; *See also* training
rockets. *See* flares
Roman Catholic service, 55–57
Rouen, 28–30
Royal family: gift from Mary R., 17

sapping, 65
servant. *See* Keekie and Jamieson
"Seventy-fives," 89
Shand, 2/Lt. A., 42, 66
shells, nicknames of, xxii, 38
shelling, British: at Aubers Ridge, 97–98; at Neuve Chapelle, 86–87; by "Mother," 128; increased capacity of, in June, 109; fatal results of short-fall, 127
shelling, German: allegedly deteriorating, 78, 82; at Neuve Chapelle, 86–90; at Le Touret, 89; lyddite, 119–20; shrapnel, 109–10
shopping: at Boulogne, 29; at Le Havre, 7, 9; at Lillers, 50; at Ordnance Stores, 27; at Southampton, 1–2
singing: and drinking, 22–23
Skene, Capt. P. G. M., 38
sniping, British, 81; by Merrilees, 76; company practice, 55
sniping, German: danger from, 75, 84–85, 99; near Dead Cow Farm, 92–93; of high caliber, 79; role in practice attacks, 68–69; telescopic sights, 82
snow, 24, 54, 66–67, 70–71, 94
soccer, 63–64
Sotheby, Lionel: characterization, xviii–xx; family, xv–xvi; attendance at Eton, xvii; joins up, xviii; injures his thumb, 26, 38; visits father at Boulogne, 30–31; reaches the front line trenches, 75; supports the advance at Neuve Chapelle, 81–90; attacks at Aubers Ridge, 97–102; is trapped in no man's land, 98–102; is transferred to 2nd Battalion, Black Watch, xxi; is transferred to 1st Battalion, Black Watch, xxi, 34; returns to 2nd Battalion, Black Watch, xxiv, 116–17; enters the trenches at Mauquissart, 123; advances at Loos, 135–38; goes missing, 138
Sotheby, William (Lionel's father): at Boulogne, 30–31; war service, xvi
souvenirs: cartridges, 104; collected from dead

Germans, 130; German helmet, 124; miscellaneous, 125; shell fragments, 88–89; unexploded bomb, 115
Stewart, Lt. Col. C. E., 49
Swan, Lce. Cpl. D., 101, 104

tents: collapse of, 5; flooded, 18
Times, 96
Tommy, characterization of, 15–16
Tortoni's (Le Havre restaurant), 7, 9
training: mock trench attack, 57–58, 61–62, 68–69; revolver practice, 57; rifle shooting practice, 57; trench digging, 11–12, 61, 63
trains: hospital, 30; Le Havre to Harfleur, 7, 9–10; Le Havre to Rouen, 26–29; Rouen to Boulogne, 30
transcription, principles guiding editor, xxv

trenches: at Choquaux described, 74; at Mauquissart described, 123–24; draining of, 69–70; first experience in, 75–80; general description, 8; muddy conditions in, 8, 129–30; swampy terrain of, 82
tunnelling, 64–65
Tyson, J. D. and A. B, 28

Vieille Chapelle, 128

Wainwright, 140
"Wait and See" policy, 69
Wallace, 2/Lt. J., 101
Wauchope, Major A. G., 35, 119, 137–38
Williams, P, letter of, 106
Wilson, Sergt. Major W., 127, 137
wounds: self-inflicted, 16